THE IRISH LANGUAGE

An Overview and Guide

THE IRISH LANGUAGE

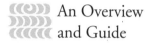 An Overview
and Guide

Darerca Ní Chartúir

AVENA PRESS

NEW YORK

Publisher:
Avena Press,
PO BOX 1502
Canal Street Station
New York, NY 10013

Editing and book design by Nikki L. Ragsdale.
Set in Adobe Garamond, ITC Tiepolo,
and Everson Typography Duibhlinn, by One Source Graphics.
Printed in the United States of America by Thomson-Shore.

ISBN 0-9670778-2-6

11 10 09 08 07 06 05 04 03 02   10 9 8 7 6 5 4 3 2 1

Contents

APPENDIX –

Student Essays on their Experiences
at Summer School

PREFACE

This book is intended as an introduction to the Irish language world. It is written for people who are studying Irish, as well as for anyone who is interested in knowing more about the place of the language in Ireland's past and present. Speakers of Irish may also find the information it contains useful and interesting.

When Irish and other small-population languages are in the news, the story is usually about loss of speakers and shrinkage of territory. For Irish, this is certainly not the whole story because, as a result of the work of restoration carried on throughout the twentieth century, a solid base now exists that the present generation is using to great effect. Confident parents are selecting schools for their children in which Irish is the medium of instruction. Many poets, novelists, playwrights, songwriters and journalists are choosing Irish as their medium. The powerful communication tools of radio, television and the internet are being fully utilised by Irish speakers. There is a greater worldwide interest in Irish than ever before, and with the good economy that Ireland is now enjoying there is reason to hope that the decline has stopped and that Irish will continue to grow in strength in the new century.

In this brief outline, readers will learn of changes and developments in the country and the language during the past two millennia, the approximate era of the Irish language in Ireland. In addition, they will find valuable information on the status of the language today – areas in which the greatest concentrations of speakers are to be found, which organisations promote Irish, descriptions of many books available in Irish or in bilingual format, publications helpful to those wanting to learn the language, descriptions of other books about the language, a selection of related web sites, locations of summer language schools for adults, and more.

The appendix contains essays by several students who attended summer schools in Ireland and wrote of their experiences for this book. Their accounts will be useful for people planning their first trip and will encourage others who may not have known that such schools exist.

THE IRISH LANGUAGE

An Overview and Guide

Introduction

In Ireland at the time of writing there are between 40,000 and 50,000 people whose first language is Irish, the majority of whom live in parts of Donegal, Galway and Kerry (all counties along the western coast), with smaller numbers in Cork, Waterford, Mayo and Meath. Because of migration from these areas, many Irish speakers can also be found throughout the rest of the country, especially in the cities. All Irish speakers are also fluent in English.

Due to emigration there are also many first-language speakers of Irish living in other countries. Celtic linguistics scholar Kenneth Nilsen gave the following estimates in 1998. In that year 20,000 speakers were dispersed throughout England, another 20,000 in the United States and about 2,000 each in Canada, Australia and continental Europe.

In addition to Irish-as-first-language speakers, it is estimated that there may be 800,000 people throughout Ireland who have studied Irish and speak it as a second language. As well, students and speakers of Irish as a second language are present in all the countries mentioned above.

Taken together, these facts should give assurance to learners that there will be plenty of opportunities to speak Irish.

1 GROWTH OF THE LANGUAGE
Irish in Ireland up to the 16th Century

THE EARLY LANGUAGE

Irish is a Celtic language belonging to the Indo-European family of languages. During the fourth and third centuries BCE the Celts inhabited areas stretching from the Carpathian mountains in east-central Europe to Ireland and Iberia. They gradually lost their continental territory to Germanic and Latin peoples, and with the loss of territory their languages declined there.

The Celtic languages of Ireland and Britain fall into two groups: Goidelic and Brythonic. Goidelic comprises Irish Gaelic (spoken in Ireland), Scots Gaelic (spoken in Scotland) and Manx (spoken in the Isle of Man), while the Brythonic group comprises Welsh (spoken in Wales), Cornish (of Cornwall but no longer spoken), and Breton (spoken in Brittany).

Although there is archeological evidence of people in Ireland before the coming of the Celts, so far it is not known what languages they spoke. It is now thought that Celtic-speaking people were dominant in Ireland by 300 BCE. Apart from archeological evidence, our knowledge of the pre-Celtic inhabitants of Ireland comes only from the ancient oral tradition, which was preserved in writing from the sixth century onwards.

THE STORY OF IRISH

The story of Irish can be roughly divided into three periods: a period of growth, followed by one of destruction, and then one of reconstruction. The first lasted until the seventeenth century, Irish being the language spoken by the majority in Ireland. There were several foreign invasions up to this time, but none did lasting damage to the status of Irish. Although the second period was a brief three hundred years, it saw Ireland being changed from an Irish-speaking country to a predominantly English-speaking one. There was always organised resistance to this loss of culture, but it did not become visible until the 1870s, when the process of conservation and renewal became open and public. This third era of Irish is still in progress and gaining in strength.

In Ireland language change usually followed the political turmoil that ensued from invasions by speakers of a different language. Readers will find accounts of these events in any general history of Ireland; one such work is *The Peoples of Ireland* by Liam de Paor. The author, an archeologist and historian, traces the social, cultural, religious and political development of Ireland from earliest times to the twentieth century. *The Course of Irish History* edited by T. Moody and A. Martin, containing essays by historians specialising in specific eras, is another standard history.

Most of the scholarly writing on the language is in Irish, including the recent 900-page history of Irish, *Stair na Gaeilge.* For a scholarly work in English, *The Irish Language* by Máirtín Ó Murchú is the best choice. In three sections, 'Political and Social History', 'Varieties of Irish' and 'Irish Grammar, Spelling and Script' the author presents a wealth of information in a short, beautifully illustrated work, using maps, charts, samples of text and reproductions of pages from the manuscripts to show the growth and change that Irish has undergone up to the present.

EARLY IRISH-LANGUAGE WRITING

The earliest known writing in Ireland is in Ogam script, in which twenty symbols composed of strokes and dots represent the sounds of the spoken language. Examples of this alphabet dating from the fourth and fifth centuries can be seen in carvings on stone, wood and bone in the collections of the National Museum in Dublin and on standing stones, often called Ogam stones or *galláin,* throughout the Irish countryside. The writing consists mostly of memorial inscriptions to important personages, as one would find on public sculpture today. The language during the time of the Ogam writings is classified as Archaic Irish, the precursor of Old Irish. *A Guide to Ogam* by Damian McManus shows that in addition to its value to scholars studying the development of the language, Ogam writings are the earliest and, in some instances, the only source of Irish personal and tribal names.

Written Irish has undergone many changes. Philologists describe four periods in its development: Old Irish (700–950), Middle Irish (950–1350), Early Modern Irish (1350–

1650) and Late Modern Irish (1650–the present). A clear demarcation line cannot be placed between one era and the next as each period developed from its predecessor, and the language and literature of each period owe their existence to the earlier forms. Old Irish and Middle Irish can now be understood only by specialist scholars.

Until the fifth century, a sophisticated oral culture existed in Ireland. The centres of learning were under the jurisdiction of Druids, the priests of the religion of Celtic Gaul, Britain and Ireland. The Romans wrote of them that they worshipped in forest groves and caves and could foretell the future. In their schools the *filí* (poets) were trained in law, history, genealogy, place-lore and speech arts. They were the designated guardians of traditional knowledge, which was systematically transmitted from generation to generation.

The first foreign intervention suffered by the Celts in Ireland occurred in the fifth century, when bands of missionaries arrived to Christianise the country, and its effects were soon felt among the learned and religious class. A conflict ensued between the newly arrived Christians and the druidic priests, which resulted in the Christian monks taking over many of the religious functions of the Druids. Although Christianity superimposed itself upon native Pagan tradition, it did so without destroying the status of Irish as the vernacular. For several hundred years Irish Gaelic schools and monastic Latin schools continued to function side by side as prestigious centres of learning. The monks wrote in Latin, but by the end of the sixth century they also wrote in Irish. Although their writing principally involved making copies of religious manuscripts in Latin, they also served as scribes to the learned class in native Irish society, transcribing material that was previously transmitted orally.

POETRY

In the earliest poetry the professional poet of the sixth and seventh centuries eulogised his patron, listing his good qualities and accomplishments and the illustrious history of his family. In the eighth century there was a change in style and new themes were introduced, and although the writing is still anonymous, the personal voice of the writer can be identified.

The poetry of the eighth century was composed by monks, who wrote it in the margins of the Latin manuscripts they were transcribing. Their themes were mainly religious, but birds, animals, plants and the beauties of nature were also favourite subjects. A poem from this period, about the writer and his cat *Pangur Bán* (White Pangur), has touched the imagination of every generation of readers because of its timelessness. The poet observes himself and his cat, each going about his special craft, one pursuing knowledge and the other hunting mice. Another much-loved poem is one in which a hermit tells the king why he chooses to sleep outdoors rather than in the palace, describing in detail the beauty of nature surrounding him. The king's answer is in the last verse, where he admits that the hermit has made the better choice.

Both of these poems can be found in *Early Irish Lyrics* by Gerard Murphy, a poet and a renowned scholar of Old Irish. This bilingual volume in Old Irish and English contains monastic and secular poems written between the eighth and the end of the twelfth centuries. While the introduction and extensive notes on each poem will be of interest to students of Old Irish only, the general reader will take great pleasure in the translations of the poems.

TRADITIONAL KNOWLEDGE OF PLACES

Writing on place figures prominently in the manuscripts, both in prose and in verse. The name may refer to legends that have been associated with the place or to its physical features, such as a ridge, an elevation, a well, a tree – especially an oak or a blackthorn (or a bird or animal that inhabited it). This literature is part of the manuscript tradition from the eighth to the fourteenth centuries and is of continuing interest to linguistics scholars and historians.

LAW TRACTS

Although the earliest available manuscripts containing law tracts were written around the fourteenth or fifteenth centuries, scholars have concluded from linguistic evidence that they were first transcribed in the seventh and eighth centuries. The laws recorded in these manuscripts were in force in Ireland from pre-Christian times until the fifteenth century and were drawn up at the *Óenach* (fair), a regular assembly held for social, political and commercial purposes. The principal fair was the *Óenach Tailten,* held each year at *Lugnasad* (the midsummer festival, spelled *Lúnasa* in Modern Irish). It was presided over by the *Ard Rí* (High King) at Teamhair (Tara), in the central plain of Ireland in what is now County Meath.

The laws show Irish society to have been highly organised.

Rights and obligations of people at all levels of society were clearly stated, and no aspect of ownership of property, especially land and livestock, was left unregulated. Some of the legal writings have been translated, but much is still accessible only to scholars of Old Irish. *A Guide to Early Irish Law* by Fergus Kelly, the first modern work on the subject, is interesting not only as a legal text, but also as a window on Irish society until the sixteenth century.

VIKINGS

The next foreign intervention was by Viking raiders from Norway and Denmark, beginning in 789 and continuing until 1014. During this time learning and writing were disrupted, because many of the centres of learning were destroyed and countless manuscripts were lost or taken out of the country for safekeeping. When the invasions ended many Vikings stayed in Ireland, forming coastal settlements and becoming integrated into Irish life, and a number of Norse words became permanent additions to the language.

MYTHOLOGICAL WRITINGS

The eleventh and twelfth centuries were periods of great literary activity, both in the lay schools and the monasteries, and many of the early manuscripts containing history and literature date from this time. This included new writings, especially on religion and law, and also copying of existing books. Most of the manuscripts are known by the name of the place in which they were compiled, for example the *Book of Leinster,* the *Book of Ballymote* and the *Book of Armagh.*

Some contain a single text while others comprise a miscellany of history, mythology, poetry, genealogy, prayers and lives of saints. Preserved in these manuscripts are the earliest written versions of Irish mythology and accounts of great events from the oral tradition (which may be historical or mythological).

Scholars have organised Irish mythology into categories according to subject: stories of the gods, stories of the kings, stories of voyages and Ossianic tales. A professional poet had this material memorised and was expected to recite it as the occasion demanded. Since translations of the manuscripts began in the nineteenth century, the mythological writings have proved to be a rich source of inspiration for novelists, poets, playwrights and writers of children's literature, both in Irish and English.

Lebor Gabála Érenn (the book of invasions) lists and describes the mythological peoples who occupied Ireland before the Gaels, of whom the Tuatha Dé Danann were the immediate precursors. According to these stories, after the arrival of the Gaels the Tuatha Dé Danann went underground, surfacing from time to time to practice their magic on the affairs of mortals. In fantasy and children's literature they live on today as fairies and magicians. *Lebor Gabála* is also the source of information on the Celtic calendar year, which is different from the Julian calendar. In the Celtic calendar, the new year begins on November 1 with the great Celtic feast of *Samhain* (Halloween), followed by the feasts of *Imbolc* on February 1, *Bealtaine* on May 1, and *Lúnasa* on August 1. These were the dates on which the people celebrated turning points in the agricultural year.

Many stories in Irish mythology recount the adventures of

heroes who fought for their royal rulers in disputes over territory and cattle. The greatest of these is the epic saga *Táin Bó Cuailnge* (the cattle raid of Cooley, or simply, *The Tain*), a story of the envious queen of Connaught, Méabh (Maeve), and the war and bloodshed that ensue when she sends her most courageous warrior to seize a prize bull belonging to the king of another province. By doing this she intends to become her husband's equal in property. Friendship, greed, courage, violence and the supernatural combine to create a vivid action-packed drama, played out across the great central plain of Ireland.

In addition to the main story there are other related tales that together make up the epic. One that is often retold is the tale of Deirdre, who cries out from her mother's womb in the middle of a feast, prompting a Druid to predict that she will be the cause of sorrow for the group. The men want to kill her at birth, but the old king of Ulster, Conchobhar Mac Neasa, has her brought up in seclusion, intending to take her as a wife. When Deirdre comes of age she elopes to Scotland with Naoise, a young warrior. After a time the old king sends an emissary, Fergus, to ask them to return to Ireland, promising that there would be no retribution. Immediately on their return the king breaks his promise, recaptures Deirdre and has Naoise killed. After a year of mourning Deirdre kills herself, and the warrior Fergus, feeling betrayed by the king, leaves to join the forces of the king's enemy, Queen Maeve of Connaught.

William Butler Yeats and John Millington Synge wrote plays based on this story. For James Stephens it was the source of his novel *Deirdre,* and the name Deirdre has become one

of the most popular choices for girls in Ireland in the twentieth century.

Versions of *The Táin* are available both in Modern Irish
and in English. In Irish there is *An Táin,* by Eoghan
Ó Loinsigh. A version in English by the poet Thomas Kinsella
created a new interest in Irish mythology when it was published in the 1960s.

In the stories of the kings, the *filí,* who were the poet historians, created a heroic past for a king, showing his long
lineage and great deeds, thus demonstrating his right to be
ruler – a right that was often contested.

With the vast Atlantic ocean lying to the west of Ireland, it
is not surprising that the Irish manuscripts contain many tales
of voyages in search of new lands. Part prose, part poetry,
common themes describe sailing amid great danger to islands
that have beautiful women and fantastic plants and animals,
or to lands of eternal youth where there is no suffering or
death and happiness is forever. Other tales describe voyages
undertaken as pilgrimages to atone for wrongdoing. *The Voyage of Bran* and *The Voyage of Maelduin's Currach* are the tales
of this type most often translated and retold.

Fionn Mac Cumhail and his band of warriors, the Fenians,
are the heroes in *An Fhiannaíocht* (the Ossianic tales). These
tales describe a nomadic life of hunting, fishing and occa-
sional waging of war, with descriptions of the landscape and
the natural world interspersed throughout. A well-known
story from this mythology is *Tóraíocht Dhiarmada agus
Ghráinne* (the pursuit of Diarmaid and Grainne), a tale of
elopement and revenge that has far-reaching consequences
for the entire group.

There is a selection of these stories in *Seanchas na Féinne* by Niall Ó Dónaill that readers of Irish will enjoy. *Over Nine Waves* by Marie Heaney is a retelling in modern style English of selected stories from Irish mythology, and it includes a useful guide to the pronunciation of names appearing in the text.

THE ANGLO-NORMAN INVASION

Another invasion began in 1169, this time by Anglo-Normans, and with it came another era of change for the institutions of learning. Since the sixth century the Christian church had grown independent of the central church organisation on the continent, and had evolved into a Celtic institution. Eventually, this became intolerable to the central authorities and during this invasion they took the opportunity to reform the Irish church along continental European lines.

As with the previous invasion, the effect was strongly felt in the institutions of learning; almost no manuscripts in Irish exist from the thirteenth century. The reformation of the church resulted in religious writing reverting to Latin and a diminution of Irish studies in the monasteries. However, although English and Norman French were introduced into Ireland during and following the Anglo-Norman invasion, neither managed to displace Irish as the language of the majority during this period.

NEW CENTRES OF LEARNING

During the fourteenth century writers in Irish became active again, and this literary period lasted until the middle of the seventeenth century. Irish studies now passed into the hands of secular scholars. The schools of poetry, initially the preserve of the Druid priesthood and later affiliated with the monasteries, were revived under the patronage of powerful regional chieftains. The education of a poet lasted seven years, during which time he learned the formal literary language governing composition, and also history, genealogy, and mythology – all subjects in which the professional poet was expected to be proficient. The method of instruction was still oral, though Latin and Irish writings supplemented the course of study. Upon graduating, the poet was at the service of the chieftain, composing and reciting poems as the occasion demanded, be it celebrating the victories of his patron, remembering historical events, or composing elegies to lament the dead; this type of poetry is prominent in the manuscripts of the time. Poets trained in these schools also wrote personal poems and composed verse that they incorporated into the heroic and mythological tale cycles.

BIOGRAPHIES OF THE SAINTS

Medieval Ireland had a multitude of indigenous saints, and writings on their lives are plentiful in the manuscripts. An outstanding work in this literature is *Beatha Colaim Chille* (the life of Colum Cille) by Maghnus Ó Domhnaill. Colum Cille, born early in the sixth century, attained fame as a spiritual leader and his reputation as a holy man continued to grow after his death. His name has been revered down through the ages in oral and written form, even to the twentieth century. This life story was written in 1532 while Ó Domhnaill was chieftain of Tír Conaill (now Donegal) in the northwest, which was also the birthplace of Colum Cille.

In the introduction to a new English edition of the work, its editor, Brian Lacey, writes that the manuscript runs 'to nearly 100,000 words of verse and prose, written for the most part in clear, elegant Irish'. He also writes that Ó Domhnaill and his assistants consulted at least twenty prose sources located in manuscripts throughout the country in preparing for the project. The first complete transcription and translation by Celtic scholars O'Kelleher and Schoepperle was published in America in 1918. Their work is composed of facts and folklore, accounts of miracles and fantastic deeds done by Colm Cille, journeys he made, and poems written in his honour.

ANNALS

In addition to the wealth of written records dating from the fifth century and as a result of the experiences of the learned classes during the Viking and Anglo-Norman invasions, annals became an important category of writing from the fourteenth to the seventeenth centuries. In these manuscripts writers compiled chronologies and accounts of significant events in the life of the country and in the lives of the leading families. The title of the work usually indicated the subject matter, such as *Annála Ríoghachta Éireann* (annals of the kingdom of Ireland) or the place of writing, such as in *Annals of Inisfallen*. The annals are invaluable for historians, and linguistics scholars also use them to study change in the language.

It was not until the sixteenth century, a period when art and learning flourished in continental Europe, that Irish culture came under direct attack. By 1536, the English king Henry VIII had proclaimed himself head of the church in England and, in 1541, he gave himself the title King of Ireland. Soon it became apparent that Henry VIII's plan was to take control of politics, religion and culture, but despite the efforts of the official church and the state to anglicise Ireland, Irish remained the dominant language until the end of the sixteenth century. Scribes continued to write new versions of the sagas and to make translations from classical and medieval literature, and also to compose new works.

2 Decline
The 17th to 19th Centuries

THE SEVENTEENTH CENTURY

Throughout the sixteenth century the English had concentrated on gaining control of Ireland. The Irish resisted, but in 1601 suffered a major military defeat at the battle of Kinsale, in Munster, and the leaders were forced to flee the country.

Manuscripts were hidden or were taken abroad for safekeeping. The surviving manuscripts are now in special collections in Ireland and throughout the world, mainly in England and continental Europe, where scholars continue to translate them and to revise earlier imperfect translations. In addition to their importance in Irish studies, the writings in Old Irish are a valuable source for linguists studying the early development of Indo-European languages.

In response to the destruction that was taking place in the country, two major works of Irish-language scholarship were created, both of them histories of Ireland. The first was *Annála Ríoghachta Éireann,* mentioned in chapter 1, which was designed to be a complete record of Ireland's history from the beginning. Mícheál Ó Cléirigh, a Franciscan monk assisted by Fearfeasa Ó Maolchonaire, Cúchoigríche Ó Cléirigh, Cúchoigríche Ó Duigenáin and Muiris Ó Maolchonaire, travelled throughout Ireland consulting other scholars and collecting material for the work, which was written between 1632 and 1636. It documents genealogies and biographies of the kings and great families, land ownership and territorial disputes, and includes a chronology of important events. When complete, two copies were written from the original and those three were all that existed until the work was published in print in the nineteenth century.

In 1629 Seathrún Céitinn (Geoffrey Keating) also began writing a history, the second of the works mentioned above. Like the other historians, he travelled through the country collecting material, and in 1634 *Forus Feasa ar Éirinn* (known in English as Keating's history of Ireland) was complete. Keating, a priest and poet, was a gifted writer who made use of myth and legend to supplement factual material, and in the nineteenth century his book was published and became the standard history of Gaelic Ireland. It is still in print, in a dual language edition, published by the Irish Texts Society. Both of these works are still valuable sources for historians and scholars of linguistics alike.

In 1641 the Irish organised a rebellion against English rule, but it was suppressed and forces led by Cromwell proceeded to consolidate English rule in Ireland. In 1695 a series of laws were passed effectively excluding the Irish from any positions of power or ownership of lands or possessions. Although no law was formulated against speaking Irish, the effect of the Penal Laws was that most people of power and means were English-speaking, immediately making Irish a lower status language. In this period considerable numbers of people, overwhelmingly Irish speaking, were forcibly removed from their lands in the east and northeast to poorer land in the west. Their confiscated lands were given to English and Scottish colonists, mostly English-speaking, who were loyal to the English monarchy. The effect for the language was to give English a stronghold in the east and northeast, with a resultant weakening of the Irish language in those areas.

THE EIGHTEENTH CENTURY

During the eighteenth century poets continued to write, but without patrons and sometimes in danger of being charged with sedition. After the demise of the bardic schools, the poets met informally to hear the members recite their compositions, which included *caointe* (laments), *aortha* (satires), *aislingí* (vision poems), *amhráin chráifeacha* (religious songs), *amhráin ghrá* (love songs) and *amhráin deoraíochta* (songs of exile). Many of these poems and songs remained known to Irish people up to the twentieth century, and some are still in the repertoire of singers today.

Poems from this period can be found in *An Duanaire 1600–1900: Poems of the Dispossessed,* selected by Seán Ó Tuama, with English translation by Thomas Kinsella, published in 1981. The period covered is from the defeat of the Gaelic leaders in 1601 up to the year 1900, by which time English had become the language of the majority of the population. In a preface, the authors write that 'the main body of the Irish literary tradition is a closed book to all but the Irish-speaking, or Irish-reading, minority' and that they saw *An Duanaire* as 'an act of repossession'. It begins with anonymous poems of the seventeenth century and continues with well known work of the eighteenth and nineteenth centuries, ending with folk poetry. At that time, poetry was used to comment on historical and social matters that today would be dealt with in prose, so this book can be read as an historical document as well as an anthology of poetry. The work is enhanced by introductory essays on the historical background and the literary style of the period, as well as biographical notes on each poet.

Traditional laments for the dead were poems sung in a formal ritualised manner at the wake and funeral. While the form of the *caoineadh* (lament) was set, the content was specific to the individual deceased. *An Duanaire* contains some examples including one that has become a classic, 'Caoineadh Airt Uí Laoighaire', written by Eilín Dubh Ní Chonaill for her husband, who was killed by the High Sheriff of Cork as a result, the legend goes, of his refusal to give up his horse. (The Penal laws forbade Catholics to own a horse valued at more than ₤5.) This poem, which was written down from a woman's memory of it many years after it was first performed, is notable for its passionate emotion and its combination of formal literary elements with communal folk tradition.

The aisling or vision poem was a form that was present in Irish literature from medieval times, but in the eighteenth century it was written to carry a political message. In the aisling the poet has a vision in which he is visited by a beautiful woman, representing an Ireland bereft of her leaders. She enumerates the atrocities committed against her by the foreign invader who has stripped her of all her national symbols, and asks for help from countries in continental Europe that are sympathetic to her cause. *An Duanaire* has many examples of the aisling.

THE UNITED IRISHMEN

In 1791 a political group naming itself the United Irishmen formed for the purpose of ending English rule in Ireland. It was inspired by the revolutionary movement in France and sought and received military help from the French, but was ultimately unsuccessful. By this time, England had become extremely powerful due to the raw materials it extracted from its colonies and as a result of the markets for its own goods obtained in these same territories; Ireland could no longer withstand this formidable foe. Individuals within the United Irishmen strove to promote Irish, but the morale of the people was low and Irish language usage continued to decline.

The Penal laws passed in 1695 had forbidden Irish school teachers to teach, forcing them to give instruction secretly. A householder would have been penalised for harbouring a teacher; therefore, weather permitting, classes had to be conducted out of doors, concealed behind a hedge. In Irish this school was called a *scoil scairte;* in English it was known as a hedge school. Things continued like this from the end of the seventeenth century until the middle of the nineteenth. A sentry kept watch and warned of oncoming danger in the guise of a stranger or an informer, and schools had to change locations often. During the winter the teacher moved from house to house and lived on the hospitality of the people. When the laws were relaxed at the beginning of the nineteenth century, classes were taught in any type of building available. The subjects were arithmetic, Latin, Greek, history, geography and bookkeeping, depending on the knowledge of the individual teacher. Books were rare and expensive, and the common practice in the *scoil scairte* was learning by rote and recitation. According to P.J. Dowling in *The Hedge Schools of Ireland,* school books in Irish were almost non-existent, even though in 1824 more than two million people commonly used the Irish language, three quarters of whom spoke no English. In general, Latin and English were the languages promoted, because the purpose of the schools was twofold: to make students fluent in English so they could enter the economic life of the country, which was by that time conducted in English; and to prepare some to enter the priesthood. The role of the hedge schools in hastening the decline of the Irish language is yet to be fully assessed.

THE NINETEENTH CENTURY

In the year 1800 the English authorities forced through a law abolishing the Irish Parliament and decreed that Ireland would be a part of a united kingdom. During the seventeenth century English had become the language of law, politics and business; new statutes furthered this end. To be permitted to practise law in Ireland, Irish law students were obliged to spend two years of their legal studies in London. In 1831 the English government established schools they called 'National Schools', with English as the medium of instruction. In these schools the teaching of Irish was forbidden and pupils who spoke it were punished. Fearful of the influence of a European-educated clergy, in 1795 the English government helped found a college in Ireland for the education of Catholic priests.

Instruction was through English, ensuring that this would be the language used in churches throughout the country for those parts of the service not in Latin, further weakening the status of the Irish language. Some members of the Catholic clergy used and strongly promoted Irish, but they were in the minority.

With the law, education and the Church all under control, English became firmly established. By the middle of the nineteenth century, after two hundred years of deprivation and persecution, the majority of the Irish-speaking population lived in poverty, mainly in the rural areas of the western half of the country, while the English-speaking landowners, merchants, clergy and professional classes prospered, living in the cities and the towns, and throughout the country wherever the land was good. When the Great Famine occurred in 1845 it was overwhelmingly the Irish-speaking poor who were the victims. More than a million people died in the period 1845-1851, and more than a million and a quarter emigrated, many dying on the voyage. The Great Famine was an economic, social, cultural and psychological disaster for the Irish people; and for the language the loss was critical.

Emigration was mostly to England, America or Australia, all places where the ability to speak English was highly valued. Yet the areas of highest emigration were those that had the greatest number of Irish speakers. New York was one of the major centres of immigration for the Great Famine Irish, and New York historian John Ridge estimates that over fifty percent of Irish immigrants to New York in 1851 spoke Irish. Among his sources are the records of the American Protestant Society, which was active in attempting to convert the immigrants to Protestantism. Their Irish-speaking preachers reported that their sermons in Irish were received with enthusiasm by large numbers of immigrants, who welcomed sermons on any subject provided they were in Irish.

Just when Gaelic Ireland was suffering its steepest decline, scholars began to study its early literature. In the latter half of the nineteenth century, there was an intense interest on the part of scholars and the general public in antiquities of all kinds. Educated people, perhaps feeling the pace of change that was separating them from their past, became interested in archeology. In this general climate, Irish manuscripts became the focus of serious attention, and several important institutions were created. One of the earliest was the Iberno-Celtic Society formed in 1818 by a group of scholars to study and publish material from the manuscripts. In 1820 one of its members, Edward O'Reilly, published a *Chronological Account of Nearly Four Hundred Irish Writers,* in which he catalogued all Irish writers from earliest times up to the eighteenth century. This book was reprinted in 1970 with an introduction by Gearóid S. Mac Eoin in which he writes that the majority of writers chosen by O'Reilly are poets because in medieval Ireland only poets claimed authorship; writers of prose were usually anonymous. In spite of this limitation, it is an amazing achievement, and one that paved the way for scholars who came after.

In 1853 the founding of the Ossianic Society, dedicated to publishing early Irish-language manuscripts, indicated an awakening of interest in the Irish language. It was at this time that the scholar John O'Donovan (1806–1861) translated and typeset *Annála Ríoghachta Éireann,* the history that was compiled in 1636 by the five scholars mentioned earlier.

Eugene O'Curry (1796–1862), professor of Irish history

and archeology at the newly established Catholic University of Ireland, published his lectures on early manuscripts in 1861 as *Manuscript Materials of Ancient Irish History*. His lectures described the historical, genealogical and mythological writings of medieval Ireland, which made them an invaluable resource for the newly emerging field of Irish historical studies.

The Society for the Preservation of the Irish Language, founded in 1876, published many other manuscripts with translations. The Irish Texts Society was founded in 1900 to publish Old and Middle Irish texts with English translations, to make them accessible to historians and students of literature. Many of the literary treasures mentioned earlier are available from the Society; for example, *An Lebor Gabála Érenn* (the book of invasions), *Tóraíocht Dhiarmada agus Ghráinne* (the pursuit of Diarmaid and Grainne) and *Forus Feasa ar Éirinn* (Keating's history of Ireland). The Irish Texts Society remains active, continuing to publish new translations and to maintain the earlier texts in print.

Throughout the nineteenth century there were people in authority – although few – who promoted the use of Irish. One was a powerful bishop, Archbishop MacHale, who translated into Irish six books of the writings of Homer, several books of the Scriptures, liturgical hymns and the popular songs of Thomas Moore. He also wrote an Irish catechism and a prayer book. It was he who inspired an tAthair (Father) Peadar Ó Laoghaire (1839–1920) to write in Irish. In his autobiography, *Mo Scéal Féin* (my own story), an tAthair Peadar Ó Laoghaire writes that, while a student in the Catholic seminary, he was reading a prize essay before an assembly of ecclesiastical dignitaries. When he had finished, Archbishop

MacHale praised him for having written well about the writers of Greece, Rome, France, Spain, Germany and England, but noted that he had not mentioned the literature of Ireland. Because of this comment, Ó Laoghaire became interested in Irish and his fictional writings were among the first to be published during the restoration period.

In the nineteenth century, other scholars became interested in Old Irish. Johann Kaspar Zeuss, a Bavarian scholar and one of the earliest Celtic philologists, began the study of Celtic languages in 1840. He visited libraries in many European cities that had collections of Irish manuscripts and copied Old Irish glosses dating from the seventh, eighth and ninth centuries. His major work, *Grammatica Celtica* (1853), brought attention to Irish as a source for the study of Indo-European languages and their evolution.

This work was continued by other continental European scholars. Rudolph Thurneysen, a German scholar, spent a lifetime compiling a grammar of Old Irish, the first part of which was published in 1909, followed by a translation into English in 1946. D'Arbois de Jubainville, at the Sorbonne in Paris during the 1880s, brought out a translation of Irish mythological writings from Old Irish into French, mainly the stories of the Tuatha Dé Danann. During the same period in Germany, Ernst Windisch published a grammar of Old Irish and a vocabulary of Middle Irish, as well as a treasury of Old Irish writings, *Thesaurus Paleohibernicus,* which he compiled in collaboration with the Irish scholar Whitley Stokes. Kuno Meyer, another German scholar, had at least nine volumes of translations from Old and Middle Irish pub-lished between 1886 and 1913, among them *The Triads of Ireland* and a collection called *Ancient Irish Poetry.*

In the early twentieth century in America, Celtic scholars Tom Peete Cross and Clark Harris Slover produced an anthology named *Early Irish Tales.* Combining in one volume the mythological, Ulster, Fenian, and kings cycles, and the Voyages, their work brought the main body of Irish mythology to a wider public.

Through the work of these multinational scholars, the study of Old Irish became established in Ireland, Europe and the United States. Occasionally, this interest led to the study of the modern written language too, although spoken Irish was still seen as a language of the poor.

3 RECLAIMING A HERITAGE
The 20th Century

IRISH IN THE TWENTIETH CENTURY

While scholars concentrated their attentions on Ireland's heroic past and Old Irish, the living language continued to decline, with the linguistic wealth of the country being lost through continued emigration. Economic and political institutions favoured speakers of English, while the school system and the major religious establishments, Catholic and Protestant, also promoted the use of English at the expense of Irish, even in areas where Irish was the only language of the majority of the people.

In a history of Dursey Island in County Cork, a local historian, Penelope Durell, describes the decline of Irish there in the period 1850–1900. She cites census figures, which show that between 1851 and 1891 in the barony of Beara the population of 4,278 monolingual Irish speakers was reduced to 531. In the census of ten years later she shows that everyone on the island of Dursey knew both languages except the school teacher and her husband, both of whom knew only English. Census figures like these were widespread. It was not unusual to find that the teacher and the priest, often the only two people in the community with formal education and high status, were ignorant of Irish while their students and parishioners, respectively, were fluent in Irish and had minimal or no English.

But in the midst of all this loss, positive things were beginning to happen. In 1882 the first periodical in Irish was published, *Irisleabhar na Gaeilge*. In 1893 a group of young intellectuals, recognising the value of Irish, founded Conradh na Gaeilge (the Gaelic League), the aim of which was to restore the spoken and written language in Ireland through the study and publication of existing Irish literature, and to encourage new writing. The specific problems they identified were emigration of native speakers because of lack of work in their home areas, a shortage of Irish-language teachers in the English-speaking areas, and the inability of both native and non-native speakers to read and write Irish.

To implement its aims, the organisation formed branches whose main function was to give instruction in the language. Irish-speaking travelling teachers were appointed to teach young and old to read, write and speak Irish. This highlighted the need for learning materials, which led to the opening of a publications centre. One of their first publications, *Simple Lessons in Irish* by Eoghan Ó Gramhnaigh, sold 32,000 copies in 1897 alone. For Conradh na Gaeilge, the travelling teacher system was just an interim solution; its ultimate goal was to have Irish taught in the schools.

In the same year, Conradh na Gaeilge held its first 'Oireachtas', an all-day public assembly with contests in Irish-language oratory, storytelling, and song. Although there have been years in which it was not held, 'an tOireachtas', which is now several days in length, is still one of the highlights of the year in the Irish speaking world.

By 1889 there were 43 branches of Conradh na Gaeilge, seven of which were in America. A weekly bilingual newspaper was begun, the first time ever for news to be published in Irish.

The founders of Conradh na Gaeilge always realised that the lack of paid work in the *Gaeltachtaí* (Irish-speaking areas) and the resultant emigration would negate all the efforts of 'an Conradh', and support for Irish industry was part of the campaign for the language from the beginning – by promoting the manufacture of Irish goods for the domestic market and for export, and by encouraging the populace to buy Irish goods.

Progress was still being made in 1902. The first novel in Irish was published in that year, as were some collections of short stories and a play. As well, 135,000 copies of *Simple Lessons in Irish* were sold. Irish was being taught in 1,300 schools, and the first meeting of the Irish Industrial Development Association was held. In 1904 a much-needed new Irish-English dictionary was published, compiled by a lexicographer and member of Conradh na Gaeilge, Fr. Patrick Dineen. This was an important resource for the emerging generation of writers in Irish.

One of the mechanisms of colonisation in the seventeenth century and later was to change people's names, giving them English versions of their first and last names. Conradh na Gaeilge had an Irish Surnames Bill introduced in the English parliament with the object of restoring people's names to their original Irish-language forms. This encouraged many people to restore their names, although doing so brought them into conflict with the authorities, especially the Post Office. Members of Conradh na Gaeilge usually got involved in these controversies.

A major figure in the movement for restoration of the language was Douglas Hyde (1860–1949). The son of a Protestant clergyman in the west of Ireland, he was a founding member and the first president of Conradh na Gaeilge. In addition to his organisational gifts, stories he collected from the country people in his locality show an appreciation of and respect for contemporary spoken Irish that was in advance of his time. His works in Irish, written under the pen name *An Craoibhín Aoibhinn* (the pleasing branch), include plays, poetry, memoirs and retellings of stories from folklore. He also wrote in English a comprehensive study of Irish literature, *A Literary History of Ireland,* published in 1899.

In 1905 Conradh na Gaeilge sent Douglas Hyde on a fundraising tour of America, which he describes in detail in *Mo Thurus go hAmerice, nó imeasg na nGaedheal ins an oileán úr* (my journey to America, or among the Irish in the new land), published in 1937. Here he described his reception in each venue, the people he met and the amount of money he raised. In six months Hyde raised $64,000. Much of the success of the tour was due to advance planning by organisation member Tomás Bán Ua Concheanainn, a native speaker of Irish who knew America well. He traversed the continent and organised almost fifty speaking engagements for Hyde, many of which were very successful, such as the one in San Francisco, where his lecture raised over $9,000. Although the tour was a financial success, it highlighted obstacles that were looming as the new organisation became embroiled in the politics of the time.

The driving force of Conradh na Gaeilge was the secretary of the publications committee, Pádraig Mac Piarais (Patrick Pearse, 1879–1916). Educator, poet, short story writer, journalist and revolutionary, he edited the Conradh na Gaeilge newspaper, *An Claidheamh Solais* (the sword of light). He became fluent in Irish, which he learned, as did Douglas Hyde, from Irish speakers in the west of Ireland. Mac Piarais studied bilingual educational methods in Belgium, where Flemish and French were taught, and instituted those methods in the school he founded in Dublin in 1908. Around this time he became active in revolutionary politics, and this preoccupied him for the next eight years.

The battle for restoration of the language was fought on many fronts: against the National Bank, which refused to honour cheques signed in Irish; against the National Railways, which refused to put up the names of stations in Irish; and in numerous court cases involving names in Irish on commercial carts. In 1908 Conradh na Gaeilge launched a major campaign to make Irish compulsory in the new National University, and, after five years, this was achieved.

With each success the stakes got higher and the disputes – both internal and external – over bilingualism, dialects, compulsory Irish and numerous other questions, became more intense. The biggest conflict was between Douglas Hyde, who wished to keep the organisation apolitical, and Pádraig Mac Piarais, who joined those calling for armed revolution against England, and it resulted in Hyde's resignation from Conradh na Gaeilge. After this the organisation became preoccupied with nationalist politics, and for the next ten years national and international conflicts overshadowed the language move-ment. But the achievements in behalf of the language had been immense, and were there to be built upon by future generations.

Mac Piarais became commandant-general of the Republi-can army in the Irish Revolution in 1916. The British consid-ered this to be treason and executed him, along with the other leaders. His death was an incalculable loss for the language movement. Two of his works are in print, *Íosagán Agus Scéalta Eile, selected stories,* and *Rogha Dánta/Selected Poems.* Both are in bilingual editions. Douglas Hyde's contribution to Irish culture was recognised when he was chosen as first *Uachtarán na hÉireann* (President of Ireland) in 1939.

The movement for the revival of Irish was not confined to Ireland; the Irish in America were also active in setting up classes to teach the language. Micheál Ó Lócháin started Irish language classes in 1872 in New York, and in the next ten years classes were established in other cities in the United States. In 1881 Ó Lócháin founded an Irish-language monthly journal, *An Gaodhal.* It was the first such publication ever, one year before the first Irish-language magazine was pub-lished in Ireland. Working closely with Conradh na Gaeilge in Ireland, the first English branch of *'an Conradh'* was formed in London in 1896. One of its members and language teach-ers was Pádraic Ó Conaire, who is considered one of the best writers of twentieth century literature.

Modern Writing

It would take a volume many times the size of this one to do justice to every Irish language author whose creative gifts have contributed to the body of work that enriches readers today.

Poets, novelists, journalists, songwriters, playwrights and others have continued to work in the Irish language with great skill and enthusiasm, no less today than in centuries past, and modern writers have added new dimensions to the literature in Irish, reflective of the times. There are many fine published authors whose work could not be covered in these pages, but it is hoped that the following outline will give the reader a sense of the vibrance and growth of Irish language writing throughout the nineteenth and twentieth centuries, and on into the twenty-first. Hopefully, it will encourage readers to explore further the wealth of creative works increasingly available to people who love and enjoy the Irish language.

Foundations

An tAthar Peadar Ó Laoghaire (1839–1920), referred to earlier, was an important writer in this period. He chose to write in the regional speech of Munster and was very prolific, writing novels, an autobiography, plays and children's stories. Because his work was widely used as school text material, it created by default a standard for writing in Irish. His novel *Séadna* (1904), one of the earliest novels published in Irish, is still widely read. His autobiography, *Mo Scéal Féin,* has interesting historical elements including depictions of the Great Famine and the language change from Irish to English in his area of West Cork. Both works have been translated into English.

Another of the earliest modern writers in Irish was the aforementioned Pádraic Ó Conaire (1882–1928). His novel, short stories, plays and journalism gave courage and self-confidence to other writers, reassuring them that Irish could serve the needs of the twentieth century. Ó Conaire read the European writers of his time and was conscious of the growing world movement for social justice, as is evident in his journalism, but his ideas clashed with the conservatism that developed among the authorities in Ireland in the 1920s, and it was not until much later that his writing gained the readership it deserved. His depictions of the dark side of Irish emigrant life in London, the alienation of the returned emigrant and the class system in Ireland are masterful. Translated into English in 1994 as *Exile,* his *Deoraíocht* (1910) is still one of the best of the early novels written in Irish.

These four people, Douglas Hyde, Pádraig Mac Piarais, Pádraic Ó Conaire and Peadar Ó Laoghaire, writing in different styles and with very different ideologies, were the major contributors to the establishment of foundations for a twentieth century Irish-language literature.

The English publishing industry flourished in the nineteenth century and many Irish writers writing in English got their work published by English firms in Dublin or London, and exported to or co-published in America and Australia. But for Irish language publishing every component of the infrastructure on which publishing depends was missing – money, writers, readers, libraries, bookshops, reviews, publicity, and the school textbook business. A two hundred year 'war of attrition' on the Irish language had resulted in parents illiterate in Irish, unable to teach their children at home even if books had been available. In the schools there were few teachers who were fluent in the language and textbooks in Irish were scarce or non-existent. Yet, in an atmosphere of political tension that periodically escalated into a state of war, committed individuals and small groups, working largely without funds, managed to sow the seeds of a publishing industry that today is one of the success stories of the movement to restore Irish.

The extraordinary language restoration movement of 1881 to 1921 has tended to be overshadowed by the military events of 1916 to 1923. In *Prose Literature of the Gaelic Revival, 1881–1921: Ideology and Innovation,* Philip O'Leary presents the personalities of the movement and some of their debates, speeches, editorials and letters on the language question. People in small language groups all over the world, struggling daily to maintain their languages while fending off the global salesmen and media dictators, would be encouraged by reading about the work and achievements of this group. Much of their debate centred on two points: first, what form the written language should take; and second, the controversial question of subject matter.

Because of the near-obliteration of writing in Irish since the seventeenth century, literary Irish had fallen into abeyance. The choice for editors, publishers and scholars was either to create a standard form of grammar and spelling or to allow the regional spoken forms to establish themselves in writing. Whether the national literature would be influenced by other cultures or should develop only from its own roots, as they were defined in this newly postcolonial society, was a question that aroused passionate feeling. Looking back now, such concerns may seem unrealistic considering how small a pool of Irish-language writers was left after the revolution, when many of them had been either executed or put in prison, but the debate was important to the cause. These issues were eventually resolved, but not until later in the century.

In 1925 the new Government established a publishing division called An Gúm. It became very active, publishing original fiction and nonfiction written in Irish, as well as translations of English fiction into Irish. It published popular as well as literary work, with the object of providing varied reading material in the Irish language. Although authors were critical of the editorial control and culturally conservative bent of An Gúm, it must be considered a success because it laid the foundation for an Irish literature, and among the many writers it published, several have stood the test of time and have become classics.

Whatever strides the economy made in the few short years of stability after independence were cut short by the Great Depression and then by the Second World War, and the stress caused by these events slowed the language movement considerably. It was not until the 1940s, with the establishment of the independent publishing firm of Sáirséal agus Dill, that Irish language writers had a choice of publishers. The firm published some excellent literature in well-designed editions, and most of their writers were of the first generation of an independent Ireland. The founding of an Irish-language book club also helped in developing a readership, and even though the economy did not improve until the 1960s, it was a time of great hope for writers.

THE 1920S TO THE 1940S

During this time, modern Irish-language literature was dominated by three writers who were born around the turn of the century and whose reputations have not diminished with time. Séamus Ó Grianna (1889–1969) from County Donegal wrote novels, short stories and two volumes of autobiography under the pen name *Máire,* and did translations for An Gúm. In *A Reader's Guide to Books in the Irish Language,* Seosamh McCloskey writes that Ó Grianna's novel *Caisleáin Óir* is interesting not only as a novel but as a social history of the Donegal Gaeltacht at the turn of the century, with its backdrop of economic pressure and emigration.

Seosamh Mac Grianna (1901–1990), a brother of Séamus Ó Grianna, wrote works of more complexity in a very different style. His best books are *Mo Bhealach Féin* (my own way), an autobiography, and a novel, *An Druma Mór* (the big drum), published in 1972 but written much earlier. Seosamh Mac Grianna's health failed just as he seemed to be reaching his creative peak, and this was a major loss for Irish literature. A recent book on this writer, *A Flight from Shadow: The Life and Work of Seosamh Mac Grianna* by Pól Ó Muirí, places Mac Grianna at the forefront of 20TH century prose writers.

Máirtín Ó Cadhain (1906–1970), born in County Galway, is considered the most important Irish writer of this century. He wrote novels, numerous essays and six books of short stories, and also translated English-language novels into Irish. His best known work is *Cré na Cille* (the earth of the churchyard), a novel that has eighty characters who are all dead and buried in the local graveyard, but who continue to address the obsessions – personal, local, national and international – that preoccupied them while alive. Although the characters are consumed by bitterness, envy and disappointment, these qualities are always leavened with sharp humour. First published in 1939, this novel has been the focus of many studies in literary criticism, but it can also serve as a social document, showing the vibrant life of a small area of Connemara, the extraordinary variety of words and expressions available to the characters, their resilience in coping with community loss through emigration, and also revealing how they incorporated the emigrant stories of American and English life into their world view.

There are no English translations of the works of Mac Grianna or Ó Grianna. A selection of Máirtín Ó Cadhain's short stories was translated by novelist Eoghan Ó Tuairisc under the title *The Road to Bright City,* and a translation to English of *Cré na Cille* is available as a doctoral dissertation by Joan O'Keefe. Translations of *Cré na Cille* into several major European languages were commissioned by UNESCO, and more recently it has been published in Norwegian and Danish.

THE 1950S AND 1960S

The writing of this period is defined by three poets: Máire Mhac an tSaoi, Máirtín Ó Direáin and Seán Ó Riordáin.

Máire Mhac an tSaoi, born in 1922, is the first woman Irish-language poet to achieve major status in modern times. Her knowledge of classical Irish and European literature is evident in her four books, in which themes of love, tragedy and nature predominate. Many consider 'Suantraí Ghráinne' (Gráinne's lullaby), based on the Fenian tragedy *Tóraíocht Dhiarmada agus Ghráinne,* to be her best poem. Some of her poems, with self-translations, can be found in the bilingual poetry anthology, *An Crann Faoi Bhláth/The Flowering Tree,* edited by Declan Kiberd and Gabriel Fitzmaurice. Her recent poetry can be found in the Irish-language literary journals.

Máirtín Ó Direáin (1910–1988) was born on the Aran Islands off the west coast of Ireland but spent his adult life in Dublin. Although he had prose published, it was as a poet that he excelled. Psychologically, he never left Aran. He saw the city as a place with neither soul nor spirit of community, where human values eroded, and this was the subject of much of his work.

Seán Ó Riordáin (1917–1977) from Ballyvourney, County Cork, wrote several collections of poetry. His Christian philosophy inspired poems dealing with the mysteries of life and death, as did his chronic illness as a young person. Being aware of the importance of introducing children to poetry, he wrote poems for them that became favourites, especially *'Cúl an Tí'* (the back of the house) – a place which at night becomes *Tír na nÓg* (land of the young), the familiar farmyard with its domestic animals and discarded objects transformed when Aesop, the scholarly phantom, holds sway under the light of the moon. In addition to his importance as a published poet, Ó Riordáin, as guest lecturer in University College, Cork, was a strong influence on a new generation, which became the voice of Irish poetry in the 1970s and 1980s, and his prose essays in the Irish Times gave him a wide and appreciative readership.

Volumes of each of these poets are in print and selections of all of their works are included in anthologies, some with translations.

Another major figure who emerged at midcentury is Seán Ó Tuama (b.1926), a poet, dramatist, teacher and critic. In each area, his contribution is marked by the finest scholarship, combined with style and vitality. In addition to three collections of poetry and three plays, Ó Tuama produced two important poetry anthologies. *Nuabhéarsaíocht,* published in 1950, brought the work of contemporary poets to the attention of the public. *An Duanaire 1600–1900: Poems of the Dispossessed,* published with Thomas Kinsella in 1980, did the same for poets of the earlier period. His most successful play was *Gunna Cam agus Slabhra Óir* (a crooked gun and chain of gold). He also wrote two poetry studies, *An Grá in Amhrán na nDaoine* (love in the songs of the people) and *An Grá i bhFilíocht na nUaisle* (love in the poetry of the gentry). A bilingual selection of his poetry was published in 1997, ironically entitled *Rogha Dánta/Death in the Land of Youth,* with translations by the author and Peter Denman.

In 1959 Diarmaid Ó Súilleabháin (1932–1985) published his first novel, and from then until his early death he published four more novels, and plays and poetry also. He was influenced by the new literary movements of post-war Europe, and especially by the writing of Albert Camus. The evils of capitalism and the unrealised ideals of nationalism were among his themes, as was his distaste for the materialism he saw emerging in Ireland in the 1960s. His novels won many prizes. His writing style was modern, experimental and not easily accessible. None of his work has been translated into English.

Liam Ó Flaithearta, a prolific and highly acclaimed author of novels, short stories and screenplays in English, was born on the Aran Islands and was a native speaker of Irish. He became famous when his novel *The Informer* was made into a film. In 1953 his only collection of short stories in Irish, *Dúil* (desire), was published. Like his books in English, *Dúil* was an immediate and enduring success.

THE 1970S TO THE TURN OF THE CENTURY & BEYOND

Poetry

Both poetry and fiction flourished in the last third of the twentieth century. By now there was a choice of publishers eager for new writing. Poets influenced by Seán Ó Riordáin and Seán Ó Tuama at University College, Cork, in the south of Ireland began to have their work published in the late 1970s. A stylish poetry journal, *Innti,* which first appeared in 1970, focused attention on the work of Nuala Ní Dhomhnaill, Michael Davitt, Gabriel Rosenstock and Liam Ó Muirthile, all of whom have gone on to fulfil their early promise. Throughout the country the poetry of Cathal Ó Searcaigh, Biddy Jenkinson, Áine Ní Ghlinn, Pearse Hutchinson, Louis de Paor and others was being published, and public readings attracted large audiences. It was a very exciting period in the literary history of Ireland. These poets have seen their work translated, some in dual-language editions and in anthologies – mostly into English, but also into continental European languages. Although not everyone agrees that translation into English is a good idea, it certainly helps learners to read work in Irish that would otherwise be inaccessible to them, and it can be an incentive to continue studying the language.

To get better knowledge of the lively world of Irish poetry now, the reader should start with some of the dual-language anthologies such as *An Crann Faoi Bhláth/The Flowering Tree: Contemporary Irish Poetry with Verse Translation into English,* selected and edited by Declan Kiberd and Gabriel Fitzmaurice (1992), mentioned earlier. For this anthology the editors selected poetry from each generation, twenty-eight poets in all, beginning with Máirtín Ó Direáin, born in 1910, and ending with Colm Breathnach, born in 1961. Most are self-translations, and for many of the poets this may be the only translation of their work. In addition, this book has a 32-page essay on contemporary Irish poetry by Declan Kiberd, one of Ireland's foremost literary and social critics.

The Bright Wave/An Tonn Gheal: Irish Poetry Now (1986), edited by Dermot Bolger, is an anthology of poetry of the 1970s and 1980s that includes work by Michael Davitt, Nuala Ní Dhomhnaill, Cáitlín Maude, Micheál Ó hAirtnéide, Liam Ó Muirthile and Cathal Ó Searcaigh. There is a valuable 11-page introductory essay in English by the novelist and critic Alan Titley. The English-language versions of the poems, which are in parallel text, are by Irish poets who write in English.

Fiction

Some of the important writers of fiction of the last third of the century are Séamus Mac Annaidh, Pádraic Breathnach, Pádraig Ó Cíobháin, Pádraig Standún, Alan Titley, Seán Ó Siadhail and Miceál Ó Conghaile. Their styles vary widely, but all are firmly grounded in the Ireland of today, a country no longer isolated but a vital part of Europe and the modern world.

Alan Titley (b.1947) has had novels, two collections of short stories and some plays published. His subject matter ranges widely from cannibalism and moral values in contemporary Dublin to the life of a thirteenth century bardic poet, and his style and language are complex. He is also one of the most influential Irish-language critics, and his award-winning *An tÚrscéal Gaeilge* (the novel in Irish) is the definitive study of the twentieth century Irish-language novel. There are no translations of his work.

Irish writers are renowned for the short story written in English, and this art is also strong in the Irish language, best exemplified by Pádraic Breathnach (b.1942). Since 1974, six collections of his short stories and one novel have been published. A selection of his short stories was translated by Gabriel Rosenstock and published as *The March Hare and Other Stories.*

Séamus Mac Annaidh (b.1961) created a sensation with his first novel, published when he was twenty-two. In *Cuaifeach Mo Londubh Buí,* the first of a trilogy, he mines science fiction, world mythology, and Irish history, especially its slogans, to produce a work of striking originality. In planning a trilogy at age twenty he displayed tremendous self-confidence, but his subsequent three novels and a short story collection show that he was justified.

Colm Mac Confhaola's historical novel *Ceol an Phíobaire,* set in 1798, the year of the United Irishmen's revolution, won the prize for best novel in the 1996 Oireachtas. This is the second excellent novel set in 1798. *L'Attaque,* by Eoghan Ó Tuairisc, was written in the 1970s and tells a tragic story that shattered many of the myths of the glory of war. Because this novel was written in Irish, it did not receive the ecstatic reviews that Thomas Flanagan's *Year of the French* did, but at least, Ó Tuairisc's publisher has kept his book in print and that is praiseworthy.

Pádraig Standún is the most prolific novelist writing for a mass readership. His writing is direct, unadorned and plot-driven, and his novels deal with controversial social and sexual issues that have come to the fore in Ireland since the 1970s. Sales of his first novel, *Súil le Breith,* rivalled that of English-language best-sellers. Many readers found *Na hAntraipeologicals* his best (it is titled from the name given by the local people to the anthropologists who invade rural Ireland to study 'the natives'), although each novel is eagerly awaited by a growing readership. Some have been published in English translations and these also are widely read. His latest novel, *Saoire,* has as its subject matter Irish people on holiday in Greece, escaping from problems at home but still being forced to face up to unpalatable truths about their lives, without the protection of their familiar surroundings.

Among the younger generation of Irish-language writers, there are several who see the world through the eyes of young characters enmeshed in pop culture. Mícheál Ó Brolacháin has two collections of short stories, a children's story and an excellent novel, *Cá bhFuil Tú Anois* (a dark but comic story of a son's revenge for the death of his father, a failed soccer star). Eoghan Mac Cormaic's *Cáibín an Phápa,* a novel about sightings of President Kennedy, Elvis Presley and Pope John in Donegal, shows real comic flair. Ré Ó Laighléis has broken new ground in the many books he has written for older teenagers on contemporary themes such as crime, drugs and the latest music. These books are also popular with adults.

Emigration is often a subject in Irish-language fiction because it was the one constant in the Irish-speaking areas, where 'abroad' was as real as home. Colm Ó Ceallaigh's three novels, *Sclábhaíocht, Deoir Ghoirt an Deoraí* and *Brídín,* all deal with the life of recent emigrants to America and are full of adventure and conflict. Maidhc Dainín Ó Sé (b.1942) who emigrated as a young man from Kerry, first to London and from there to Chicago, is another writer who draws on the emigration experience in his novels *Chicago Driver* and *Greenhorn.* Even his novel for young people, *Is Glas Iad na Cnoic* (faraway hills are green), is about a cat who emigrates to New York and gets in with the wrong crowd. His style is realistic and exciting.

Many novels published in Irish are, like postmodern

literary fiction in Spanish, French and English, nonlinear, plotless, loaded with arcana and allusions, sometimes without a clear beginning or end, and the reader who is less than fluent might feel the need for a teacher or reading group leader. Books written in a more conventional manner, but in nonstandard Irish and full of regional idioms, present different challenges. In an effort to bridge the gap between these and children's books, publishers have created a new category of novellas or short stories written in simple language specifically for the adult learner with strong plot lines, adult themes, usually crime or mystery, and with a glossary of more difficult words. Some titles are *Dúnmharú ar an Dart* and *An Tobar* by Ruaidhrí Ó Báille; *Robáil Gan Foréigean* by Pádraig Ó Luanaigh; *An Bhean Úd Thall* by Cliona Cussen; and *An Punk agus Scéalta Eile* by Ré Ó Laighléis. These books are very popular, encouraging learners at a point where they might feel bored by children's reading material. The two most recent titles, *Dúnmharú sa Daingean* by Eilis Ní Dhuibhne and *Paloma* by Pól Ó Muirí, are excellent murder mysteries that deserve a wide readership.

Plays

Playwrights have made a significant contribution to Irish literature in the twentieth century. Máire Ní Ghráda (1899–1971), Eoghan Ó Tuairisc (1919–1982) and Seán Ó Tuama (b.1926) all saw their work produced and well received. Brendan Behan's play *An Giall* became *The Hostage* in English and it was a great success in both versions. The Irish-language version is available in print in *Poems and a Play in Irish* by Brendan Behan.

Antoine Ó Flathartha (b.1953) is the most prolific new

dramatist, writing some plays in Irish and others in English. The young Irish making the pilgrimage to Elvis Presley's Graceland, and the young American students going in the opposite direction to Lady Gregoryland, are some of the themes of his comedies.

Eilis Ní Dhuibhne had two plays produced recently, *Milseog an tSamhraidh* and *Dún na mBan Trí Thine,* both published in print in one volume by Cois Tine. She has also published a novel and stories in English. A specialist in folklore, in her writing she makes creative use of legend, history and mythology.

Anthologies and Collections

Sláinte: Deich mBliana de Chló Iar-Chonnachta, a 572-page anthology, contains short stories, excerpts from novels, poetry, songs and drama representative of Cló Iar-Chonnachta's first ten years of publishing. It is a fine selection and will surely gain new readers for the authors whose work is included.

Croí Cine: Dréachtíní agus Sleachta as Litríocht na Gaeilge, edited by Seán de Fréine, was published in 1990. The title means 'heart of the heritage: excerpts and selections from Irish literature', and in it the editor has distilled the essence of Irish writing from earliest times to the present with themes for each chapter, such as 'the flourishing of devotion', poetry, womanhood, banishment and exile, conviviality and feasting, courtship, babies, language and death. Where the selections were from Old and Middle Irish, the editor has translated them to Modern Irish. This book is a treasure.

Bliainiris 2000, edited by Ruairí Ó hUiginn and Liam Mac Cóil, is an anthology of fiction, poetry and nonfiction published to mark the millennium. The contributors include such important writers as Nuala Ní Dhomhnaill, Biddy Jenkinson, Máire Mhac an tSaoi, Séamus Mac Annaidh and Seán Mac Mathúna.

To commemorate the end of the twentieth century Cló Iar-Chonnachta published *Rogha an Chéid,* three volumes of selected writings 1900–2000. In the first, *Gearrscéalta an Chéid,* Gearóid Denvir and Aisling Ní Dhonnchadha have presented their selection of the best short stories of the century. Next, Padraig Ó Siadhail edited *Gearrdhrámaí an Chéid* to present the best short plays. Finally, in *Duanaire an Chéid,* Gearóid Denvir selected the hundred best poems of the twentieth century. In addition to providing an interesting retrospective of the period, this handsome set is a treasure for Irish book collectors. It is bound in black cloth with gold decoration, and comes in a slip case.

Books for Children

Most publishers of Irish-language books have some titles for children. The most prolific publisher of books for the young is the government-run publishing company An Gúm. It provides a complete bilingual catalogue with good descriptions, organised according to age group.

Among the many wonderful children's books published by An Gúm, both for quality of illustration and story, are Mary Arrigan's *Lá le Mamó* and Béibhinn Ní Mheadhra's *Faoi Rún.* Lucinda Jacob's *Emma and Julia* books in bilingual Irish/English, with Irish text by poet Maire Mhac an tSaoí, have beautiful illustrations and just a few lines of text with each picture, making them really inviting for very young readers.

Many successful adaptations of children's books from other

languages preserve the original illustrations while the text is translated into Irish. The *Spot* series by Eric Hill is hugely popular in Irish, just as it is in other languages. In Irish the name of the puppy became *Bran,* which was the name of Fionn Mac Cumhail's dog in mythology. Also very successful in translation are the little bear stories by Martin Waddell, especially the first book, *Oíche Mhaith, a Bhéirín.*

Some Irish-language autobiographies and novels gained an international readership in English translation, and in Ireland translations sometimes increased sales of the Irish-language editions, because they helped learners and readers of Irish who might have difficulty with regional or local idioms.

Of five autobiographical works from what has come to be known as the Blasket Island literature, three have achieved the status of classics. The Blasket Islands lie off the southwest coast of Ireland and are now largely uninhabited. Because of their location and the difficulty of access, the autobiographies describe a lifestyle that had changed less over the centuries than most other places in Ireland. The authors were all gifted in the use of language and were fortunate to have come in contact with people who appreciated their art and who were in a position to bring it to the attention of publishers.

The first of these is Tomás Ó Criomhthain, whose *An tOileánach* (1929) was published in English as *The Islandman* (1937). The author was born in 1856, so he was able to observe and describe a long era when great changes were taking place. *Peig* (1936) by Peig Sayers was published in English as

Peig: The Autobiography of Peig Sayers of the Great Blasket Island (1973), translated by Bryan MacMahon. This book complements Ó Criomhthain's work, because it shows the world of the island women. A second book by Sayers, *Machnamh Seanmhná* (1962), was translated by Séamus Ennis under the title *An Old Woman's Reflections* and contains history and folklore of the island, as well as personal reminiscences. Another work that reached a large audience was *Fiche Blian ag Fás* (1933), by Muiris Ó Súilleabháin, published in English as *Twenty Years A-Growing*. This is lighter reading than the others, because it deals with the life of the author up to his mid-twenties. The English translation was printed by a major American publisher and was a book club selection in America in the 1930s. Perhaps in reaction to the speed of industrialisation, a book describing the simple life was welcomed.

Peadar Ó Laoghaire's autobiography *Mo Scéal Féin* and his novel *Séadna* were both translated into English and were widely available in Ireland. Mící Mac Gabhann's *Rotha Mór an tSaoil* was first published in 1959. Mac Gabhann was born in 1865 in northwest Ireland in county Donegal. At that time it was the custom for male children to be hired to rich farmers in the eastern part of the country during the summer to work on saving the harvest, and his autobiography describes this experience, which began for him when he was nine. Later on he joined his neighbours in the seasonal migration to Scotland, also for the harvest, and when he was old enough he emigrated to America, working in the silver mines of Montana and then prospecting for gold in the Yukon Territory of Alaska. He returned to his native place in Ireland in 1902, where he lived until his death in 1948. He dictated his autobiography to his son-in-law, who was a folklore collector. It was translated into English and published under the title *The Hard Road to the Klondike*. Mac Gabhann's style of telling is direct and unadorned, and the story is grim and compelling.

The novel *Lig Sinn i gCathú* (1976) by Breandán Ó hÉithir created a stir when it was published, because the details of the wild life of a college student in 1949 on the eve of the proclamation of the Republic was not a usual subject in Irish up to that time. This book was translated into English with the title *Lead Us Into Temptation* (1978). Both Irish and English versions sold in large numbers and are still in print. In fact, *Lig Sinn i gCathú* was the first work in Irish to reach the best-sellers list. Flann O'Brien, better known for his novels in English, wrote one novel in Irish, *An Béal Bocht,* which was published in English as *The Poor Mouth*.

Cinn Lae Amhlaoibh, by Amhlaoibh Ó Súilleabháin, is a diary kept from 1827 to 1835 by a Kilkenny schoolteacher. It was first published in 1936–37 in a bilingual four-volume edition by the Irish Texts Society. In the 1970s selected entries from the diary were published in one volume edited by Tomás de Bhaldraithe. In English the title is *The Diary of Humphrey O'Sullivan.* The entries focus mostly on newsworthy local events, the seasons, holiday celebrations, natural history and the weather. Intermediate learners would find they could make headway in the one-volume edition, because the entries are short and the narrative is direct.

Translation also went the other way, especially in the 1930s and 1940s, when popular works of English fiction and classics were translated into Irish under the imprint of An Gúm. Among the translators were some of the major creative writers in Irish, including Máirtín Ó Cadhain and Seosamh Mac

Grianna. Unfortunately, this type of publishing was not continued and all works from that era went out of print. Recently, An Gúm began reprinting selected works from its archives.

Since the beginning of the 1980s, the small but significant category of translations to Irish from languages other than English has re-emerged. For example, some Irish poets have worked to establish relationships with their Gaelic counterparts in Scotland through visits and joint readings. *Sruth na Maoile: Modern Gaelic Poetry from Scotland and Ireland* was compiled by Michael Davitt and Iain Mac Domhnaill, in Scots Gaelic, Irish, and English to celebrate the first twenty-one years of the Scottish-Irish poetry exchange. The title is taken from the name of the body of water joining Ireland and Scotland, known in English as the Sea of Moyle.

Breandán Ó Doibhlin, novelist and literary critic, has translated several well-known French texts into Irish, in Irish-French parallel-text format. *Ón Fhraincis* has translations of French poetry from the Middle Ages to the twentieth century, with poems by Victor Hugo, Verlaine and Rimbaud among the selection. The other works are *Fabhalscéalta La Fontaine/The Fables of La Fontaine* and *An Prionsa Beag,* Antoine de Saint-Exupéry's *Le Petit Prince.*

The Irish version of Dante's *Divine Comedy,* the final volume of a lifetime's work in translation by the classical scholar Pádraig de Brún (1889–1960), was published in 1963 as *An Choiméide Dhiaga.* His other translations included Homer's *Odyssey,* parts of the *Iliad,* three of Sophocles' plays, poems by Shakespeare and some work by Corneille. All of these translations are directly from the original languages. Other Irish writers also translated works of classical and continental literature, including two versions of the *Rubáiyát* of Omar Khayyám.

An Mháthair is a translation into Irish by Máire Nic Mhaoláin (who also translated novels for young adults from Welsh) of *La Madre,* by Italian novelist Grazia Deledda. *Anonimo Veneziano* by Giuseppe Berto is translated by Pádraig Ó Snodaigh under the title *Venéiseach Éigin.* Meanwhile one of Ó Snodaigh's novels, *Linda,* has been translated to Italian by Rosangela Barone, and is published with the same title in a bilingual Irish-Italian edition. Cosslett Ó Cuinn translated *Peores que Lobos,* by Medicante Nocede, from Spanish to Irish. This adventure story is set in Texas in 1842. In *Nua Fhilíocht na Gaeilge,* poetry of Máire Mhac an tSaoi, Máirtín Ó Direáin, Seán Ó Riordáin and Tomás Tóibín was selected by Daithí Ó hUaithne and translated into Hebrew by Penina Nave. This was published in a special limited edition in dual-language format to honour Chaim Herzog, then President of Israel, who was born in Ireland and who spoke Irish.

The poet Gabriel Rosenstock has introduced many poets to Irish readers through his translations: Gunther Grass, Georg Heym and Peter Huchel from German, Francesco X. Alarcón from Spanish and William Roggeman from Flemish. He has also translated to Irish selected poems of W.B. Yeats and Séamus Heaney. *Glór Ár nGaolta* is the title given by the translator to a collection of short stories translated from Welsh to Irish by Diarmuid Ó Laoghaire. The title refers to the relationship between the two languages, namely 'the voice of our relatives'.

With the European Union's policies on minority languages, more translations and bilingual editions can be expected, introducing cultures to each other and reestablishing ties that were broken in the seventeenth century. The recent book by Michael Cronin, *Translating Ireland,* will serve to focus more attention on the art of translating and the wide-ranging implications of a process that was taken for granted until recently.

LITERARY CRITICISM

Irish novelists, short story writers and playwrights have produced an impressive body of work, especially since midcentury, and most are unknown outside the Irish-language world. Within that world, however, intense interest in literary criticism, mostly in Irish, has been stimulated by a healthy publishing industry. In the past, Philip O'Leary contributed a review in English on a selected Irish-language novelist to each issue of the *Irish Literary Supplement* (published from Boston College by the American Conference on Irish Studies) and these reviews are well worth searching out.

A number of literary journals in Irish, in addition to publishing essays of literary criticism and book reviews, also serve as outlets for new short fiction and poetry. In fact, these journals are where many writers get their start. Two of them, *Comhar* and *Feasta,* are for a general readership, having essays on politics and social issues in addition to fiction and poetry. *Innti,* a previously mentioned poetry journal, publishes the work of new and established poets and also carries critical essays and in-depth interviews with poets on their writing. Its nonfiction counterpart, *Oghma,* has been an excellent vehicle of literary and social commentary, succeeding an earlier journal, *Scríobh.* A third generation of literary and social criticism has now appeared under the title of *An Aimsir*

Óg, a book-sized journal that shows signs of being even better than *Oghma.* Both *Innti* and *An Aimsir Óg* are beautifully designed and are published annually. In another journal, *Irisleabhar Mhá Nuad,* the editor Pádraig Ó Fiannachta has been publishing many new voices among poets, essayists and critics.

Recently there has been an increase in full-length studies of individual Irish writers. Mairtín Ó Cadhain, Seán Ó Riordáin, Diarmuid Ó Súillabháin, Eoghan Ó Tuairisc and Nuala Ní Dhomhnaill are among writers whose work has been discussed in single volumes.

In 1991 *An tÚrscéal Gaeilge* (the Irish novel) by novelist Alan Titley was published as a history and assessment of the Irish-language novel, a summary of almost a century of novel-writing in Irish. The 631-page study reflects the author's belief that the novel is the cornerstone of a literature, a belief not shared by all in Ireland, where poetry holds a preeminent place. Since the completion of this study, at least forty more novels have been published.

Stair Dhrámaíocht na Gaeilge, 1900–1970 by Pádraig Ó Siadhail is a study of Irish-language drama. This scholar and novelist has also edited the collected plays of Pádraic Ó Conaire. Gearóid Denvir's collection of essays, *Litríocht agus Pobal* (1997), is an important addition to the critical literature. Most of the essays are on the work of twentieth century writers. Denvir is also a contributor to the *American New Hibernia Review,* writing there in English on aspects of the Irish language. Finally, the publication of Breandán Ó Buachalla's *Aisling Ghéar* (1997), a comprehensive 800-page study of Irish poetry of the Jacobite period in its historical context, has cast new light on seventeenth century history.

In *Changing States,* a critical work on the major Irish writers, novelist and scholar Robert Welch has included essays on two Irish-language writers, Mairtín Ó Cadhain and Seán Ó Riordáin. The *Oxford Companion to Irish Literature,* edited by Welch, has many entries on Irish-language writing and writers, especially of the early period.

NONFICTION

There are many interesting works of nonfiction available in Irish. A few examples include: *Ag Coimeád na Síochána* (keeping the peace) by Páid Ó Súilleabháin, which describes the professional life of an Irish policeman, a life that is not quite as it appears to outsiders. *Loingseoir na Saoirse* by Pádraig de Bhaldraithe is an account of a journey made by Conor O'Brien round the world in 1923 in his sailboat 'Saoirse'. *An Bád Chonraí go Meiriceá* by Colm Dubh Ó Méalóid describes a journey in an open boat from Ireland to Boston in 1986. *Turas Éireann* by Lorcan Ó Treasaigh is a well-written travel guide to Ireland, useful for Irish people and foreign visitors alike. In *Camchuairt Calypso,* Conor Ó Riain recounts a journey he made off the beaten track in some of the countries of the Caribbean, more as a traveller than as a tourist seeking entertainment.

Written in the 1950s but now, unfortunately, out of print, are three travel books by Úna Ní Mhaoileoin, *Turas go Túinis, Le Grá Ó Úna* and *An Maith Leat Spaigetí.* The pen and ink drawings, unsigned and apparently by the author, are as original as her witty observations and writing style. It is sometimes possible to find used copies of these books.

Ceo Meala Lá Seaca by Míchael Mac Liammóir, actor,

scholar and national treasure, is a diary of his travels in Ireland and in other countries with Dublin's Gate Theatre. Whether in Rome, Chicago, Berlin or Killarney, everywhere he went he met the most interesting people and his book is full of gossip and vivid commentary, especially on the stress of working with Orson Welles. Mac Liammóir loved the Irish language and wrote three other books, *Lá agus Oíche, Diarmaid agus Gráinne* and *Oícheanna Sidhe,* a bilingual collection of stories for children. He also wrote an introduction to Padraic Ó Conaire's *Deoraíocht,* in which he describes a meeting with the writer, for whom he had the highest admiration.

In *Féara agus Bánta Éireann,* P.L. Curraoin, an agricultural scientist, describes the grasses of Ireland – over a hundred of them, with a drawing of each one – and gives the name of each grass in Irish, English and Latin. As varieties of grasses become extinct because of pesticide and chemical fertiliser use by farmers and builders of golf courses, this book will serve as a record of what was lost.

Many novelists and poets in Ireland work as journalists and collections of their work have been published, ensuring that good writing has a life longer than twenty-four hours. Breandán Ó hÉithir was as well known as a journalist as he was as a novelist, writing a column in Irish at different times for the major national dailies, and for the journal *Comhar.* A selection of his articles was published under the title of his column, *An Chaint sa tSráidbhaile* (the talk in the village). *An Peann Coitianta* (the ordinary pen) is the title of a selection of articles that appeared in the *Irish Times,* written by Liam Ó Muirthile, poet and novelist. Two volumes of selections of these articles have been published under the same title.

Although emigrant life has figured often in Irish-language fiction, *Rotha Mór an tSaoil* by Micí Mac Gabhann and *A Thig, Na Tit Orm* by Maidhc Danín Ó Sé are among the few nonfiction works to have come out of this experience. As is to be expected, the list of history titles is extensive, added to by the recent commemoration of the Great Famine. The economic historian Cormac Ó Gráda had two books published in Irish on the subject, *An Gorta Mór* and *An Drochshaol: Béaloideas agus Amhráin.* Television producer Cathal Portéir had a book of essays by historians Joseph Lee, Kevin Whelan, Gearóid Ó Tuathaigh, Cormac Ó Gráda and others published in a book called *Gnéithe An Ghorta,* on different aspects of this catastrophic event.

With inequality in society greater than ever, Andrias Ó Cathasaigh, the London-born socialist scholar, has written two timely books, *Karl Marx, a shaothar agus a shaol* (the life and work of Karl Marx) and *An Modh Congaileach: cuid soisialachais Shéamuis Uí Chonghaile,* which presents James Connolly's views on socialism for Ireland.

Eolaí Póca is the Irish version of a series of well-illustrated pocket field guides to the European natural world that has been published in each language of the European Union. The series is a boon to the smaller language groups, which could never afford such a high quality of production. Some of the subjects are birds, mammals, fish, rocks and minerals, trees, and weather, all in an attractive set – a definite collectible.

The foregoing is just a small sample of Irish-language nonfiction and does not mention any of the growing number of books being published in Irish that are not specific to the Irish experience – on topics such as health, food, science and the natural world.

The *English-Irish Dictionary*, compiled by scholar Tomás de Bhaldraithe, was first published in 1959. This 864-page dictionary was welcomed as an authority for new terminology and as a source for the newly standardised language.

Until 1978, Patrick Dineen's *Foclóir Gaedhilge-Beárla*, published in 1904, with enlarged editions in 1927 and 1934, had been the most complete Irish-English dictionary available. In addition to being a lexicographer, Father Dineen was a poet, novelist, medievalist and translator. *An Foclóir Gaedhilge-Béarla* is still widely used, especially by poets and fiction writers who wish to enrich their work. It is kept in print by the Irish Texts Society in the same elegant Gaelic typeface as the original.

The decision of the authorities to change from the Irish-language type (*an cló Gaelach*) to Roman type (*an cló Rómhánach*) in the 1950s necessitated a dictionary to reflect this change. In addition, Dineen's dictionary lacked some mid-twentieth-century terms, especially in science and technology. Therefore, in 1959, Niall Ó Dónaill began to compile a new Irish-English dictionary, which he completed in 1978. The 1,309-page *Foclóir Gaeilge-Béarla*, sometimes referred to as *'Foclóir Uí Dhónaill'*, is one of the treasures of the Irish language world. This work was enhanced in 1994 when a version of the dictionary was published for computer. By typing in a word and pressing a key, one can obtain the meaning and all the grammatical forms of any word. And unlike the printed version, which is Irish-English only, the computerised version also permits the reverse, English-Irish. This project was conceived and funded by Pádraig Ó Maoilréanaigh from Donegal, who emigrated to the United States along with his parents when he was very young. When he decided to learn Irish in the 1990s and found that a dictionary was not available for computer, he undertook to have one produced.

In addition to the comprehensive dictionaries, the Government publishing company An Gúm also publishes many specialised dictionaries. These are essential for writing in science and technology.

Another important reference work is *Stair na Gaeilge* (history of the Irish language), edited by Kim McCone, Damien McManus, Cathal Ó Hainle, Nicholas Williams and Liam Breathnach, and published in 1994. The 900 pages of text contain essays on Old, Middle and Modern Irish, dialects, orthography, standardisation and other aspects of the language. The editors and contributors are among the foremost scholars in Celtic studies. This work is for students who are fluent in Irish and have a knowledge of linguistics.

Beathaisnéis 1782–1881 and *Beathaisnéis 1882–1992*, compiled by Diarmuid Breathnach and Máire Ní Mhurchú, make up a six volume biographical dictionary of over nine hundred people who were active in the Irish language world in writing, teaching or language politics and who are now deceased. This social history ensures that people who contributed to the life of the language will be remembered.

In Scríbhneoirí na Gaeilge 1945–1995, Seán Ó Cearnaigh gives biographies of more than 240 contemporary writers with titles of their works. This is an invaluable desk reference for students, journalists and other researchers.

Eolaire Chló Iar-Chonnachta de Scríbhneoirí Gaeilge, edited by Gearóidin Ní Nia, was published in 1988 and provides valuable information towards a 'Who's Who' in Irish-language writing.

For the Irish-language entries in the *Oxford Companion to Irish Literature,* edited by Robert Welch, more than forty Irish-language scholars contributed concise essays on writers, publishers and significant organisations.

Ár bPaidreacha Dúchais (our native prayers) compiled by Diarmuid Ó Laoghaire, S.J. contains a selection of prayers and blessings from the Irish-language tradition for every occasion. An tAthair Ó Laoghaire credits the Irish Folklore Commission with great foresight in collecting this material before it was too late.

A new translation of the Bible, *An Bíobla Naofa* was published in 1981 under the auspices of Cardinal Ó Fiach and An tAthair Pádraig Ó Fiannachta.

4 Cultural Context

HANDWRITING AND TYPOGRAPHY

Irish handwriting, based on the Latin alphabet, was in use almost unchanged for a thousand years. In the seventh and eighth centuries the scribes not only copied the sacred books and non-religious manuscripts, but also ornamented the pages and decorated the margins with elaborate interlaced designs. The scriptorium was an important section of the monastery where copying of the scriptures and other religious writings took place. The *Book of Kells* immediately springs to mind, but no less beautiful are the *Book of Durrow* and the *Book of Lindisfarne*. (It should be noted that the language of the sacred books was Latin, written in Irish script.) A less elaborate style – albeit the same script – was used in Irish handwriting and in the printing of books in Irish until the middle of the twentieth century.

In the sixteenth century the adverse political situation and the advent of typesetting diminished the honoured status of the scribes, but typesetting did not change the style of the letters. *Aibidil Gaoidheilge agus Caiticiosma* by Seán Ó Cearnaigh, an Irish primer of religion published in 1571, was the first book in Irish to be typeset in Ireland. A reproduction of this work edited by Brian Ó Cuív, published in 1994 with introduction and notes, shows this first typeface to be a work of art, a worthy development out of the manuscript tradition and as readable as if it had been created in the twentieth century. Many other Irish-style fonts followed and most books published up to the middle of the twentieth century used this elegant style. As for handwriting, it continued as it had been from earliest times, no longer the preserve of the scribes, but belonging to all who wrote in Irish. Until 1958, students in the Irish school system used the Irish style when writing Irish-language material and Roman style for anything in other languages.

The invention of the typewriter created new possibilities for Irish script, but with a few obstacles to overcome. Irish has two diacritical marks not available on the Roman-style typewriter: a length mark or accent (the *síneadh fada*) over vowels; and a dot (the *séimhiú*) over certain consonants. The length mark was not a problem, because many languages have this symbol, but the dot over some consonants was a different matter. Special keyboards were constructed for Irish, as for other languages with symbols not widely used, but the small number of keyboards that could be sold made the price very high. By 1958, therefore, the authorities decided to get rid of the dot and replace it by inserting the letter h after the affected consonants. At the same time, the traditional style of forming the letters was discarded and the Roman type was substituted overall.

The Irish font is now readily available on computer, but forty years ago this could not have been foreseen. It can still be found in Dineen's *Foclóir Gaeilge-Béarla* and also in the computer version of the Ó Dónaill dictionary, and many people still prefer to use this script in private correspondence. In fact, you can still find editions of many books printed in this beautiful lettering. As with Roman fonts, there are versions available with slight differences.

Below is one example of the Irish alphabet in a computer font (the font is Duibhlinn, part of the Celtscript set by Everson Typography), compared with a Roman font. The font contains the letters jkqvwxyz, which are not used in the Irish language itself, but are useful for printing words from other languages. Note also that there are two versions of lower case 'r', 's' and 'sh', to correspond with Irish style.

The Irish letters below are shown with their variations, and in upper and lower case. Lower case Roman style letters are given beneath them as a guide to help the reader identify letters that have a different form in Irish.

Modern Computer Font in Irish Style

ᴀᴀᴀ́ᴀ́ bbḃḃ ccċċ ꝺꝺḋḋ eeéé ꝼꝼḟḟ
a, á   b, bh   c, ch   d, dh   e, é   f, fh

ᵹᵹᵹ̇ᵹ̇ h ıíí j k l mmṁṁ n ooóó ppṗṗ
g, gh   h   i, í   j k l   m, mh   n   o, ó   p, ph

q Rʀɼ Ssſṡṡ́ ccċċ uuúú v w x y z
q   r   s, sh   t, th   u, ú   v w x y z

There are two excellent books on the art and history of Irish scripts and fonts, *The Book of Kells* by Bernard Meehan, and *The Irish Hand* by Timothy O'Neill. As well, a few addresses to web sites where Irish fonts can be obtained are given in this book on page 90.

Until the 1940s the main Irish-language publisher was the government company, An Gúm. The establishment in the 1940s of Sáirséal agus Dill, on the foundation built by the activists of the literary revival, was the beginning of trade publishing. This firm published in well designed editions the works of major contemporary writers, including Máirtín Ó Cadhain's novel and short story collections. No significant competition appeared until An Clóchomhar was founded in the 1970s with a strong list of fiction, literary biography and literary criticism. Clódhanna Teoranta, a division of Conradh na Gaeilge, became active again in the 1960s and published a diverse selection of material. Foilseacháin Náisiúnta Teoranta, unfortunately now defunct, for many years published nonfiction with an emphasis on history and historical biography.

New companies continued to start up along with the emergence of new young writers. Two of the most active, Coiscéim and Cló Iar-Chonnachta, which began publishing in 1980, have continued to grow. Both have varied and interesting lists, about equal in the amount of fiction, poetry and literary criticism, and they both publish some of the best contemporary writers. Coiscéim publishes fiction writers Séamus Mac Annaidh and Pádraig Ó Cíobháin, and the poet Biddy Jenkinson. Cló Iar-Chonnachta publishes the fiction of

Pádraic Breathnach, Micheál Ó Conghaile, Pádraig Ó Siadhail, Seán Ó Siadhail and Pádraig Standún, and the plays of Antoine Ó Flathartha. Coiscéim's nonfiction includes many titles on the movement for Irish independence, including biographies of participants. In addition to its literary titles, Cló Iar-Chonnachta emphasises popular culture. The company is located in the centre of an Irish-speaking area in County Galway and is very supportive of the culture in the region, publishing the work of local songwriters and producing numerous recordings on tape and CD.

The literary journal *Comhar* also publishes fiction and essay collections. Selections from the first writings of many an established writer have appeared in this journal. Though still small, the new companies Cois Life and Leabhar Breac have each created a strong presence in the publishing world – the former with the work of Liam Ó Muirthile and the stories of Sean Mac Mathúna, the latter most notably with the novels of Liam Mac Cóil.

A 1995 survey of Irish publishing by Coopers and Lybrand showed that there were ten publishers that year whose entire lists were in the Irish language, with a further five publishing in both languages. Supporting the publishers is Áisínteacht Dáiliúchán Leabhar (ÁIS), a book distribution agency founded in 1978 by Bord na Gaeilge, the government organisation established in the 1970s to promote the use of Irish. It carries almost three thousand titles and ships Irish-language books to booksellers in Ireland and all over the world. ÁIS is highly regarded by both publishers and book shops for the promptness and efficiency with which it fills orders and for ensuring that booksellers are informed about new books.

Indeed, writing and publishing have been the most

successful components of language restoration up to now. Looking back to the beginning of the twentieth century, the view of what has been accomplished by Irish-language publishers in such a short time is truly admirable. They have built a solid foundation for the future.

FOLKLORE

The earliest Irish and Irish-Latin writings of the Middle and Early Modern Irish periods are rich sources of tales recited by the *seanchaí* (storyteller). Their unwritten stories were passed down through the ages and many would have been lost were it not for the establishment in 1927 of the Folklore of Ireland Society and its journal, *Béaloideas* (oral tradition). Collection and conservation of this oral tradition were begun informally towards the end of the nineteenth century by a group of people who were alarmed at the continued decline in the Irish-speaking population and who felt that their rich story tradition was worth saving.

In 1930, the Society became the Irish Folklore Institute, and later the Irish Folklore Commission (1935–1971). Director Séamus Ó Duilearga organised the gathering of material by full time collectors, who were stationed in different parts of the country. These collectors were residents of the areas, who knew the local speech and history and were able to contact the best storytellers.

Collection was accomplished both by writing down what was told and by recording it, the latter proving to be more valuable as the language becomes more standardised, since recordings preserve the actual sound of the speech of the various regions. Material from the collections is published occasionally, sometimes in dual-language versions.

In 1937 and 1938 a collection scheme was carried out in all the National (primary) Schools throughout the twenty-six counties. School children, using specially prepared guidelines, collected stories from their elders on such topics as local history, sport, superstitions, customs, songs, prayers, riddles and tales of the supernatural. This resulted in a vast amount of information from areas where no collecting had been done before.

Material was collected in the dominant language of each area, and all of the Irish-speaking regions were represented. The original collection in the pupils' handwriting, with the names of the collectors, the informants and the place collected, is housed in the manuscript archive and departmental library in University College, Dublin, where it is accessible to scholars and members of the general public. Major parts of the collection are available on microfilm at various third-level institutions in Ireland. For certain areas, the Schools' Collection can be consulted in county libraries and some have been published. This material is valuable for learners because, while the narrative is simple and charming, the language is natural and rich in idiom. Indeed, it is vastly richer in idiom than a comparable collection would be today. It would be suitable as supplementary reading for learners at the intermediate level.

The Department of Irish Folklore at University College, Dublin, now undertakes the collection, classification, and study of all aspects of Irish folk tradition in Irish and English, and teaches the subject at undergraduate and postgraduate level. Many publishers have collections of folklore on their lists.

When Ireland gained its independence in 1922, the Constitution declared Irish to be the national language and the new government introduced many programmes aimed at making this statement a reality. They were only partially successful, because the country was in an economic depression until the 1960s and funding for language programmes was never adequate. This was most evident in the severe shortage of the vital element in second language acquisition: qualified teachers. Even though there was an organised system of education it was based on an English model, and not enough teachers in the system knew Irish when the 1922 Government declaration on Irish was made. Even so, Irish was added to the curriculum and the teachers were expected to teach a language while trying to learn it themselves. Lack of funding also prevented adequate continuing education in the language for adults. Other factors apart from lack of funds stood in the way of success, but this was the most crucial.

With a better economy prevailing in the 1970s, Bord na Gaeilge was founded as the state body responsible for coordinating the work of all Irish-language agencies and for the promotion of Irish as an everyday community language. Bord na Gaeilge fulfilled this role through the end of the century, when a new all-island body was set up as part of a peace accord between the Nationalists and the Unionists in the north of Ireland. This new body, Foras na Gaeilge, offers great promise for the future of the language as it fosters the strong bonds already existing between the Irish-language groups north and south. The responsibilities and staff of Bord na Gaeilge, An Gúm (the previously mentioned government publishers) and

An Coiste Téarmaíochta (committee for terminology development) were all transferred to the new body. By the time of writing, Foras na Gaeilge has become a fully operational cross-border institution, continuing to provide the support put in place by Bord na Gaeilge.

Among the organisations supported is Comhar na Muinteoirí Gaeilge, which provides further education for Irish-language teachers. Also supported are the *Gaelscoileanna*, schools in which pupils are instructed through the medium of Irish. These schools were founded in the 1970s, in response to parents' concern that Irish language instruction in the existing schools was inadequate. *Gaelscoileanna* begin as privately funded bodies and, when enrolment reaches a certain number, they receive funding. This programme is considered to be very successful.

Among the many valuable programmes sponsored is a document translation service for state agencies, with a simultaneous interpretation system for people who wish to conduct bilingual meetings and seminars. Another innovation is a specialised dictionary of food-related terminology that has been distributed to encourage the use of Irish in hotels and restaurants. Foras na Gaeilge also gives support to Institiúid Teangeolaíochta Éireann, which concerns itself with the study of language and linguistics, with an emphasis on Irish.

Foras na Gaeilge's responsibility is to promote, facilitate and encourage the use of Irish as a living language in the Republic of Ireland, as well as in the north of Ireland wherever there is sufficient demand. To this end its roles include advising the administrations of both North and South, as well as public bodies and other groups in the private and voluntary sectors, on all matters relating to the Irish language, and, as stated above, continuing the work of Bord na Gaeilge, An Coiste Téarmaíochta and An Gúm. It provides support and funding to a wide range of Irish language organisations, events and activities, such as workshops, training seminars, and Irish language education; development of new terminology in Irish; the compilation and publication of Irish-language dictionaries; production, distribution and promotion of Irish-language and Irish-interest books, guides and resource materials; advertising, competitions, launches and exhibitions; and sponsorship of bilingual events.

Areas in which there is a concentration of people who speak Irish are known as *Gaeltachtaí,* and are to be found in counties Donegal, Galway, Mayo, Kerry, Cork, Waterford and Meath, as well as in Belfast and Derry in the north of Ireland. Statistics give the Irish-speaking population of the *Gaeltachtaí* as about 50,000. In recent times, maintaining the language in Gaeltacht areas was recognised as vital for the country as a whole, and a number of special government agencies were established to promote and strengthen their economic, social and cultural development. The coordinator of these agencies is Údarás na Gaeltachta (the Gaeltacht authority), which takes an active role in encouraging businesses to locate in the Gaeltacht communities and in promoting tourism in these areas.

An Chomhairle Ealaíon (the Arts Council) is the public body responsible for development of the arts in the Republic of Ireland. To promote the Irish language, it provides sponsorship for creative artists in music, literature and drama.

In 1997, Bord Scannán na hÉireann (the Irish Film Board) and Teilifís na Gaeilge (the Irish language television station) together established a programme that provides funding to support and help Irish language writers and directors. This scheme is called *Oscailt* (open) and its aims include adding to the body of short films in Irish and encouraging new talent in all areas of Irish language drama production.

Gael Linn has been engaged in activities to promote the language for over forty years. In the area of entertainment it has produced high-quality recordings of the best Irish singing and traditional instrumental music. *Slógadh,* an arts festival, is the flagship of Gael Linn's youth activities. This annual festival gives first-time public performance opportunities to over 15,000 young people from all 32 counties of Ireland. The groups Clannad and Hothouse Flowers had their early performances at these events. Gael Linn also sponsors scholarships, organises summer schools in the *Gaeltachtaí,* and conducts debating competitions in second and third-level learning institutions. It also sponsors live radio quizzes in Irish.

IRISH IN THE NORTH OF IRELAND

For purposes of government administration, Ireland is divided into thirty-two counties, nine of which are located in the northern part of the island in the province known since ancient times as Ulster. In this book, the term 'the north of Ireland' refers only to six of these nine, the counties of northeast Ireland that are governed by England and are often the subject of world news because of conflict between the two major communities there. The status of Irish there is not the same as in the Republic of Ireland. In broadest terms, descendants of the English and Scottish people who came to the area in the seventeenth century favour retaining union with England (they are often called Unionists), while

Nationalists, who tend to be descendants of the original inhabitants of the area, favour either independence or a reunion with the twenty-six counties of the Republic. Language is sometimes one of the contested issues.

Until the seventeenth century Irish was the language of most of the inhabitants of northeast Ireland. With the influx then of a large number of English-speaking people, who replaced the Irish-speaking inhabitants, use of the Irish language declined. By the beginning of the twentieth century there were just small isolated groups of Irish speakers left.

When the Irish-language restoration movement began at the end of the nineteenth century, it was active throughout the entire country. After the war for Irish independence, a treaty was signed leaving England in control of the six northeast counties of the nine counties of Ulster. The Irish language was reinstated as the national language in the twenty-six counties of the Republic, but in the six northeast counties it had no official status. While it was not forbidden, Irish was in many ways discouraged in the north of Ireland, although it was taught in schools managed by the Catholic church. Volunteer organisations persevered with the restoration movement by providing continuing education classes in Irish and by using the political process to demand rights for the language. They have made some important gains: Irish is now taught at all levels throughout the region where there is a demand for it. In addition, two universities offer degree courses in Irish. Among published Irish-language writers, an impressive number come from this region. The community has a high-quality weekly Irish-language newspaper, *Lá,* and some programming in Irish on BBC Radio Ulster; people are now working towards increasing Irish on television. With the turn-of-the-century peace talks, Irish is one of the areas in which cooperation between the peoples of the north of Ireland and the Republic of Ireland should be of great benefit to both groups.

More information on this topic can be found in *The Irish Language in Northern Ireland,* edited by Aodán Mac Póilin.

IRISH IN EVERYDAY LIFE

Names

Many Irish personal, family and place names are of Irish language origin and are the most obvious indication to visitors that English is not the only language in Ireland. Some names have retained their Irish spelling, while others may be spelled according to English spelling rules.

Personal Names

The personal names in use in Ireland make a fascinating study – the most commonly used names in one period falling into complete disuse in another, usually coinciding with the dominant culture at the time. In their excellent book, *Irish Names,* Donnchadh Ó Corráin and Fidelma Maguire tell us that at least twelve thousand names have been in use in Gaelic, according to the annals, genealogies, and mythological and historical tracts. Under English dominance, many Irish personal names were replaced by English, biblical and classical names. They were replaced again in the nineteenth century by continental European saints' names, in the case of Roman Catholics.

From *Irish Names* we learn that *Mór,* meaning 'tall, great' was the most popular name for women in late medieval Ireland. Yet in 1881, according to John Ridge's *Immigrants from 'The Irish Nation' 1882,* by far the most common name for Irish women emigrants arriving in New York was Mary, followed closely by Brigid, Catherine and Anne. By 1991 these names would be only rarely given. In fact, in Ireland of the 1980s more Irish Gaelic names were given than at any time since the Middle Ages.

Patrick Woulfe's *Irish Names for Children* lists not only Irish Gaelic names from medieval times, but also English, biblical and saints' names in their Irish-language versions, such as *Eilís* for Elizabeth and *Éamonn* for Edward. Ó Corráin and Maguire's *Irish Names* contains about a thousand names, with fascinating information on their mythological and early historical origins. The book by Woulfe gives shorter histories but has more names, especially Irish translations of English ones.

One of the most popular Irish Gaelic names now in use is *Émer,* beloved of Cúchulainn, hero of the great Irish myth *The Tain.* She is described as being beautiful, wise and sweet-spoken. *Órla* (*ór* means gold), was the fourth most popular name in the twelfth century and was used by many of the powerful families. It fell out of favour in the later middle ages, but has found new life since the mid-twentieth century. Many Irish kings were named *Fergus,* after the mythological warrior Fergus mac Róich in *The Tain.* The name had almost died out by the nineteenth century, but is very popular again. *Ailill* was one of the most popular names in early Ireland, both in mythology and history, and is being used again, although not commonly. In mythology it is found in the

Ulster Cycle, and in history among powerful abbots and warriors. Some early Irish names were almost exclusively the preserve of specific families, and many of those developed into the Irish family names of present times.

Many Irish-speaking people are better known in their native areas by modifications of their given names. For example, the name of a parent or some other important person in an individual's life may be added, resulting in names like *Seán Mháirtín* (Martin's Seán) or *Séamus Mháire Tom* (Tom's Mary's Séamus). Unofficial names may be added to official ones in combinations like *Tom Bheairtle Tom Ó Flatharta*, the storyteller from Indreabhán in Connemara, and *Peadar Sheán Shiúnac Mhac Conaola*, the poet from Inis Meáin in the Aran Islands (who is also known more simply as Peadar Mór). Other names may come from an individual's characteristics, such as *Úna Rua* (redhaired Úna) or *Máirtín Óg* (young Martin, or Martin Junior). Names such as these are usual in fiction set in Irish-language areas; Máirtín Ó Cadhain's novel *Cré na Cille* has many examples.

Nowadays, Irish place names such as Erin, Tara and Shannon are often used by people of Irish heritage outside Ireland, as are the names Colleen, which is an Irish word for girl (*cailín*), and Alannah, which comes from an Irish word for 'child' (*leanbh*). These names are not common in Ireland.

Family Names

The prefixes *Mac, Mc, Ó* and *O* are very common in Irish surnames. The Irish word *mac* means 'son', and the abbreviation 'Mc' is often used in English. For the officials who translated the names into English dropping the middle 'a' saved time, paper and ink. Breandán Mac Diarmada translates literally to Brendan, son of Dermot, but is written in English as either Brendan MacDermot or Brendan McDermot.

The prefix *Ó* (note the accent) is a word in Irish, not just a letter of the alphabet; it means grandson or descendant. This was transcribed into English as O, which, lacking the accent, has no meaning. *Ó Néill* came to be written as O'Neill.

In Irish, there are usually separate prefixes for female and male. The feminine of *Mac* is *Nic* as in *Bríd Nic an Bháird* (anglicised as Brigid Ward), and *Ó* is *Ní* as in *Máire Ní Chonchubhair* (Mary O'Connor).

Ó and *Mac* were often dropped from Irish surnames during colonisation, under pressure to assimilate to English norms. Beginning in the second half of the nineteenth century, Irish people began to restore these prefixes. The movement to go further and return to original given and family names in Irish is gaining strength.

One of the best sources of information on family names is Edward MacLysaght's *Surnames of Ireland*. The names are listed alphabetically in English, followed by the original Irish-language spelling and a brief history of the name with its most frequent geographical occurrence. Dr. MacLysaght spent a lifetime studying surnames in consultation with the leading historians and scholars of Old and Middle Irish.

Place Names

Many place names in Ireland, though written in English, often sound like Irish because in fact, that is what they are. In the play *Translations* by Brian Friel, the officer of the English army's Ordnance Survey must rely on the translator, a local person who speaks both Irish and English, to pronounce the place-names of the district, so that he can write them phonetically in English on his map. This method was used throughout the country in the first half of the nineteenth century. Whether something approaching the original sound of the place names was achieved depended on the skills of the individual who transcribed them.

Some common prefixes are: Kil-, Bally-, Rath-, Knock-, Dun-, Letter-, Clon-, Gort-, Inis- and Derry-. Frequent suffixes are -beg and -more. As the following list shows, all were originally actual Irish-language words.

Baile (a town) became Bally as in:
Baile an Chaisleáin 'the town of the castle' – Ballycastle

Ráth (a fort) became Rath or Rah, as in:
Ráth Eoghain 'Eoghain's fort' – Rathowen
Rath Éanna 'the fort of Enda' – Raheny

Cnoc (a hill) became Knock as in:
Cnoc na gCapall 'hill of the horses' – Knockacappul

Dún (a fortress) became Dun or Don as in:
Dún na nGall 'the fort of the foreigner' – Donegal
Dún Laoghaire 'the fort of Laoghaire' – Dunlaoghaire

Áth (a ford) A shallow place in a river was very important for transport, and towns grew up around these fords, giving us names such as:
Áth Lúain 'Luan's ford' – Athlone, Co. Westmeath, on the River Shannon.

Cluain (a meadow) became Clon:
Cluain Meala 'the meadow of honey' – Clonmel

Gort (a cultivated field) remained Gort:
Gort an Choirce 'the oats field' – Gortahork

Doire (a wood, especially oak) became Derry:
Doire na n-Éan 'the wood of the birds' – Derrynane

Leitir (side of a hill) became Letter:
Leitir Ceanainn 'Ceanainn's hillside' – Letterkenny

Inis (an island and also land beside a river):
Inis Mór 'the big island' – Inishmore
Inis Fada 'the long island' – Long Island
Inis Ceithleann 'Island of Cethlenn' – Enniskillen

Beag, mór (small, big) became beg and more:
An Charraig Bheag 'the small rock' – Carrickbeg
Trá Mhór 'the big beach or strand' – Tramore

Many of the meanings of place names have been lost because their origins in Old or Middle Irish are unclear or the topographical features that led to their names have disappeared over time. The subject has been of interest to Irish-language scholars since the nineteenth century, and as Old Irish scholarship progresses, new and more accurate translations become available.

There are two excellent reference books on place names. The *Gazetteer of Ireland* was prepared by the Place Names Branch of the Ordnance Survey and gives the principal geographic names of Ireland, with cartographic, linguistic and grammatical information in bilingual format. In *Irish Place-Names,* Deirdre Flanagan and Laurence Flanagan explain the origin and derivation of the names of over 3,000 cities, towns, villages and townlands.

Official Titles and Public Signs

When Ireland regained its independence in 1922, restoration

of Irish was a primary aim and many titles, offices and public places were given Irish names, and public signs written in Irish.

Following are some titles and offices recurring most often in newspapers:

An Rialtas – the government

An Dáil – the parliament, also means an assembly

An Taoiseach – the Prime Minister, also means chief or ruler

An tUachtarán or *Uachtarán na hÉireann* – The President, or President of Ireland (Uachtar can mean cream, head or upper part)

Áras an Uachtaráin – the residence of the President

Aire Stáit – Minister of State

Ceann Comhairle – Speaker. Means 'Head of the Council'.

Fianna Fáil – a political party. Translates as 'soldiers of destiny'. The term derives from Irish mythology.

Fine Gael – also a political party. Translates as 'race or family-group of Irish people'.

Teachta Dála (TD) – a member of parliament. Teachta means 'messenger' and Dála means 'of the Dáil'.

Tánaiste – Deputy Prime Minister (heir apparent)

Gardaí Síochána – Police force (Guardians of the Peace), often called the *Gardaí* in speech and in the press. A *garda* is a policeperson.

Here are some of the most common Irish-language public signs encountered by the visitor to Ireland:

Iarnród Éireann – Irish Railways
Busáras – the Bus Station
An Lár – City Centre
Mná (Women) and Fir (Men) – for restrooms
Ná Caitear Tobac – No smoking
Dúnta – Closed
Ar Oscailt – Open
Fáilte – Welcome

Street names are usually given in both Irish and English, and common traffic signs are written in Irish in the Gaeltachtaí.

Singing in Irish

Some very successful singers and groups perform songs in Irish, in both traditional and contemporary styles. Many of them come from Irish-speaking areas, and for many people all over the world, hearing these singers was the first time they had the opportunity to hear Irish.

One of the first traditional singers to become known outside Ireland was Seosamh Ó hEanaí (Joe Heaney). He emigrated to America and in the 1970s began performing and teaching the art of stylised unaccompanied singing, known in Irish as *amhránaíocht ar an sean-nós* (singing in the old style) or simply *sean-nós*. This art is very highly developed in Connemara, County Galway, where Heaney was born. He gave performances before small select groups and also conducted classes. His singing was recorded, but not often, and only in the latter part of his life. He never reached mass audiences, but his name is revered among people who appreciate the art.

In the 1980s, the Ó Domhnaill and the Ó Braonáin families from County Donegal gave a visibility to Irish that it never had before. They performed new original songs, as well as old songs, in both traditional and modern arrangements, with exquisite instrumental music. Tríona and Mairéad Ní Dhomhnaill performed with their brother Micheál in the group Skara Brae, before going on to build solid reputations as soloists. Eithne Ní Bhraonáin sang with her sister Máire on Clannad's early albums and went on to win worldwide fame as a soloist under her new name, Enya. This Donegal tradition has been continued by the group Altan, with their fiddler Máiréad Ní Mhaonaigh, who also sings in both Irish and English.

Many artists are finding the Irish language to be a satisfying vehicle for their more contemporary approach as well. For example, singer and song writer Tadhg Mac Dhonnagáin has recorded songs that range from a rocking blues style to tender love ballads to a wonderful collection described by Mac Dhonnagáin as 'songs for children and former children'. His insightful lyrics are infused with both humour and compassion, and a sense of the beauty as well as the irony of life. Another example is the band Kíla, whose distinctive fusion of traditional and contemporary rhythms in their original music and song (which they describe as Nua Traditional, *nua* meaning new), is finding a wide appeal in an audience of modern listeners who appreciate this style. There are many examples to be found by perusing the music shops and catalogues, even country-and-western style singing and hip-hop.

Two recording companies, Gael Linn and Cló Iar-Chonnachta, produce a great many of the Irish-language recordings now available and both have large lists of traditional and contemporary singers from all regions.

Social Irish

In recent years a growing number of Irish language gathering places have blossomed around the country, including in cities outside the Gaeltachtaí such as Dublin, Cork, Limerick and others. In these establishments Irish speakers can meet socially in an atmosphere conducive to using their Irish. They include restaurants, cafes, cultural centres, clubs, bookshops with meeting areas or cafes, and the like. Menus and other materials are in Irish, servers speak Irish, and most of the customers do as well. In 2001 Foras na Gaeilge produced a booklet, *Ré nua don teanga* (a new era for the language), that contains details on such places, as well as a lot of other useful information. They will be happy to provide copies of that or similar future publications upon request. See 'Some Helpful Organisations', page 114, for contact information.

SPOKEN IRISH: REGIONAL VARIATIONS
AND THE STANDARD LANGUAGE

Until the seventeenth century there was a standard literary language for Irish writing. After the dispersal of the literary class, and especially as large English-speaking groups came to separate Irish-speaking areas from each other, the Irish language became regionalised with almost no intermingling of the people of the Irish-speaking regions. Since change is constantly taking place in spoken languages, the language in each area developed its own unique changes leading to the variations in dialect found in the country today.

To meet the need for a standard Irish in schools and in government documents, two publications were issued. The first was *Litriú na Gaeilge: Lámhleabhar an Chaighdeáin Oifigiúil* (Irish orthography: the official standard handbook), published in 1945. This was followed in 1958 by *Gramadach na Gaeilge: An Caighdeán Oifigiúil* (Irish grammar: the official standard). The publication of dictionaries followed.

The three main regional varieties of Irish are those of Ulster, Connaught and Munster. Standard Irish is closest to that of North Connaught. To speakers of the language, all are mutually comprehensible because their similarities are much greater than their differences. However, the regional variations can seem an obstacle to beginners, and experts would suggest that the learner choose any one and become competent in that form. As all are equally valid, a reason for choosing one regional variety over another could be ancestral or family ties to a specific region, preference for one region as a holiday place, the regional speech of the language learner's teacher, or a favourite textbook.

As would be expected from the distance that separates them, there is a noticeable difference in pronunciation between Ulster (north) and Munster (south) Irish. Connaught (west/ middle) is closer to Ulster from the point of view of phonetics. To give just a few examples, in words like *cnoc* (hill), and *gnáth* (usual), the 'n' is pronounced as spelled in Munster but in Connaught and Ulster it is pronounced 'r', i.e., *'croc'* and *'gráth'*. The letter combination 'ao' as in *naomh* (saint) is pronounced *'é'* (ay) in Munster and *'í'* (ee) in Connaught and Ulster. A word ending in 'igh', like *mínigh* (explain) for example, is pronounced 'meeNIG' in Munster but in Connaught and Ulster people say 'MEENee' (or 'MEENuh'). The final syllable of a word like *glacadh* (acceptance) is pronounced 'uh' in Munster and Connaught, 'oo' in Ulster.

The most conspicuous difference in pronunciation among the regions involves word stress or accent. In the Irish of Connaught and Ulster, the stress is normally on the first syllable of a word. In Munster, however, the stress is shifted to another syllable if there is a long vowel sound in the word.

Munster	Connaught / Ulster
cail*ín* (girl)	*cail*ín
fuin*neog* (window)	*fuin*neog
siopa*dóir* (shopkeeper)	*siopa*dóir

Some words are used in one region but not in another. For example, *ní* is the usual word for 'is not' in Irish, but in Ulster it is *cha* or *chan* that are often used instead:

Ní *rún é, nuair is fios do thriúr é.*

Chan *rún é, nuair is fios do thriúr é.*

(It is not a secret when it's known to three people.)

NEWSPAPERS, RADIO, TELEVISION,
THEATRES & FESTIVALS

The first weekly newspaper in Irish was *An tÉireannach,* begun in 1934. It was independent and it focused on news from the Irish-speaking areas, as well as the failure of trade policies, the growing threat of fascism in Europe, and imperial politics in the European colonies. It was the most progressive paper ever published in Ireland in either language, but it survived only until 1937.

The next Irish-language weekly, *Inniu* (today), was published from 1943 until 1984. In a letter to a friend from his home in England, the playwright Seán Ó Casey wrote of *Inniu* that it brought one closer to Ireland than any of the three national English-language daily papers. It was a serious, well-produced paper, and its demise points to a problem that languages with small populations face all over the world, which is that one newspaper can never satisfy all the different requirements within a society. In the 1980s it was felt in some policy-making circles that *Inniu* was too serious to appeal to youthful readers, and it was replaced by a tabloid, *Anois* (now), which seemed to many to be only for the young. In 1997 *Foinse* (source), a new weekly paper, was founded, and this time it appears that a happy medium has been reached. It covers local, national and international news, the literary and visual arts, popular music and sports. It has a circulation of approximately 7,500. As mentioned previously, another weekly Irish-language newspaper, *Lá* (day), is published in Belfast. While its emphasis is on the north of Ireland, *Lá* also covers national and international news. The editor of its excellent arts section is Séamus Mac Annaidh. The high quality of the photography in both *Foinse* and *Lá* give the papers a very lively appearance in print. As well, both *Foinse* and *Lá* have been available to read on the Internet for some years now. (Their web addresses are given on pages 96 and 111.)

The national radio station (RTÉ) always had some Irish-language programmes, but Irish speakers felt that an all-Irish station was necessary. In the 1960s a group of activists organised a civil rights movement that led in 1972 to the founding of an all-Irish radio station, Raidió na Gaeltachta (RnaG), now national in scope, but with special emphasis on the regions where Irish is still the first language. It provides a comprehensive news service that includes international, national and local news, news analysis and current affairs, as well as music, light entertainment, sports, quizzes, and educational and religious programmes. Through the Internet, RnaG can now be heard worldwide via a live stream available from the web sites of RnaG and RTÉ. RTÉ's web site also provides an excellent, regularly-updated archive of daily and weekly RnaG programmes, available for download from its site so that listeners in distant time zones can now hear programming they might otherwise have missed in the live stream. (For URLS to these and other media mentioned in this chapter, see pages 90-97.)

A second radio station, Raidió na Life (Liffey Radio), serving Dublin and the eastern region, was begun in 1993 with sponsorship from Bord na Gaeilge. It is organised as a co-operative with three full-time employees and over a hundred volunteer workers. Its programme schedule is available on its web site.

The most sought-after medium of all, an Irish-language television station, came on the air in 1996. It started with five hours of service a day, since expanded to twelve hours. Great hopes were placed in Teilifís na Gaeilge as a strengthening and uniting force for the communities of speakers heretofore separated from each other geographically, and as a stimulus for speakers and learners throughout the country. It is succeeding beyond what anyone had hoped, not only because it is Irish presenting itself, although that is not to be discounted, but because it involves a well of talented young people, fluent in Irish and schooled in film and media arts, who create programmes that have a freshness and originality while simultaneously including elements of the local and familiar. The station, often called TnaG, was recently renamed TG4. Its web site provides visitors with programming information and schedules, in both Irish and English formats.

With the exception of the excellent films of Bob Quinn, there are very few Irish language films available on video for sale outside Ireland. This is a disappointment for students of Irish abroad who have found film a great help when learning languages. However, technology will soon make it possible to receive Irish language television worldwide, breaking down the last barrier to a totally connected world.

In spite of the high cost of staging plays for small audiences, the Irish speaking population is reasonably well served with live theatre. The renowned Galway city theatre, An Taibhdhearc, founded in 1927, is still active and continues to maintain a high standard in its productions. Visitors who want to see Irish-language theatre should start looking out for announcements in the newspapers *Foinse* and *Lá* well in advance of their visits. An Comhlachas Náisúnta Drámaíochta (national drama association) encourages playwrights by organising festivals of new Irish language plays throughout the country, staged by local theatre groups.

The principal voluntary organisation promoting the Irish language is still Conradh na Gaeilge (the Gaelic League), which was founded in 1893. It has 180 branches in Ireland and twenty in other countries. The organisation is active in promoting the teaching of Irish and its use in schools and in daily life, and also on national radio and television. Usually the branches outside Ireland also run language classes and serve as information centres on the language. Many of them have web sites, through which they can be contacted.

In 1897 Conradh na Gaeilge organised the first *Oireachtas* (assembly), a day-long festival of cultural events in Irish. This has grown to become the premier festival of the Irish-language world, and until the 1990s it lasted ten days and was attended by thousands of Irish speakers. All aspects of the culture were showcased at the Oireachtas including *sean-nós* (traditional solo unaccompanied singing), choral music, storytelling, competitions for new literary works, plays and dance. Many people who later became successful in the arts had their first performances at this festival. *'An tOireachtas'* was held in late autumn in a different area of the country each year. In 1996 the site was Donegal, in the northwest; in 1997, it was Belfast in the northeast; and in 1998, it was held in the southwest, in Kerry. Recently the format of the festival was changed from a ten-day event to a two-weekend one, each weekend to be held at a different location. Adults from abroad who are learning Irish enjoy attending the Oireachtas, many reporting what an exhilarating experience it is for them to be among crowds of people speaking Irish. Music, dance and art exhibitions are also showcased.

IRISH AND THE INTERNET

When the Internet began to come into wide use in 1995 and 1996, Irish-language sites became popular straight away. Until then, outside Ireland, and especially away from the big cities, people who knew or were learning Irish could go for years without coming into contact with another person who spoke the language. To find someone who spoke Irish and who shared one's interests was even harder. That is no longer the case. New web sites, mailing lists, newsgroups and chat rooms are appearing faster than any publication can keep track of them, and anything written about Irish in the Internet world is bound to be out of date before it can get into print. What can be said is that for a language population as dispersed as the Irish, nothing greater could have been invented. Speakers are no longer isolated or dependent on luck or chance to make contact with other speakers. Just type in 'Irish Gaelic' or *'Gaeilge'* and choose from a menu of riches previously beyond imagining. The response on one search engine to a request for 'Irish Gaelic' offered 2,804 web pages. The content of these varied from excellent to silly, but the overall experience was a positive one.

Using the Internet, it is now possible to get help in learning the language, to join a group based on one's special interests, or form an advocacy group to promote the language, to mention just a few of the benefits. And at the time of writing, the Internet is still in its infancy.

Following is a small selection from the many web sites available that are of interest to Irish learners and speakers:

http://www.udaras.ie/
Údarás na Gaeltachta, the agency with responsibility
for the economic, social and cultural development of
the Gaeltacht regions, to ensure continuation of the
Irish language as the spoken language of the community
in these regions.

http://www.comhdhail.ie/
Comhdháil Náisiúnta na Gaeilge provides a range of
support and advisory services to ensure that all voluntary
Irish language organisations work towards a common aim.

http://www.forasnagaeilge.ie/
Foras na Gaeilge, the all-island body responsible
for promotion of the Irish language.

http://www.dcu.ie/fiontar/
Fiontar is an Irish-medium degree program at Dublin
City University that teaches computer science, entrepre-
neurial skills and a European outlook to Irish-speaking
students. See one of the places where the future of the
language is being made!

http://www.intercelt.com
A site that provides detailed and up-to-date information
on cultural holidays, events and educational matters of
interest to Irish learners and speakers. It is supported by
Comhdháil Náisiúnta na Gaeilge. Very useful for anyone
planning to visit Ireland.

http://www.iol.ie/~leabhair/tablabac.html
Sraideanna Bhaile Átha Cliath (the streets of Dublin),
a comprehensive listing of Irish street names of Dublin.
The names are arranged alphabetically in English, the
Irish name beside each one, with notes in some cases.

http://www.evertype.com/
http://www.sil.org/computing/fonts/lang/Celtic.html
http://www.fainne.org/gaelchlo/
All three of these sites provide Irish computer fonts.

http://www.iol.ie/~sefton
Kay Uí Chinnéide's colourful website contains basic
lessons in Irish and other material.

http://www.daltai.com
This, the elaborate website of Daltaí na Gaeilge (students of the Irish language), contains phrases (some with recorded pronunciation), news on Irish-language weekends in North America, as well as discussion forums in Irish and English.

http://www.lincolnu.edu/~focal
There is something for everyone from beginners to fluent speakers at this and related sites constructed by Dennis King.

http://www.solaseireann.com
A beginner's course in Irish is offered at this site, owned by Traditional Irish Culture Ltd. in Dublin.

http://www.mis.ucg.ie/International_Office/
Summer_School/IrishLanguage.html
Summer courses offered by National University of Ireland, Galway, at Áras Mháirtín Uí Chadhain, An Cheathrú Rua (Carraroe) in the heart of the Connemara Gaeltacht.

http://www.egt.ie/
The firm of Everson Gunn maintains this site containing literature, computer games and other software in Irish, and information relating to their work with Irish and other languages.

http://www.cnag.ie
The site of Conradh na Gaeilge in Dublin. You can find other branches by doing a search online.

http://www.oideas-gael.com
Oideas Gael offers Irish-language courses and cultural activity holidays for adults. It is situated in Gleann Cholm Cille (Glencolumbkille) and Gleann Fhinne (Glenfin), in southwest Donegal.

http://members.nbci.com/crannog/
An Chrannóg is situated in Gaoth Dobhair (Gweedore), in northwest Donegal. It offers Irish Language Courses for Adults, with special emphasis on the Ulster dialect.

http://www.rathcairn.com/
Áras Uí Ghramhnaigh. Language courses and cultural holidays for adults in the Ráth Cairn Gaeltacht, County Meath.

http://www.corca-dhuibhne.com/oidhreacht.html
Oidhreacht Chorca Dhuibhne provides Irish conversation and heritage courses. It is found on the Dingle Peninsula in the Corca Dhuibhne Gaeltacht of County Kerry, in the south-west of Ireland.

http://www.gaeilge-comhchoiste.com/
Dáil Uladh, Comhchoiste na Gaeilge. Residential summer courses held in the Gort an Choirce Gaeltacht, County Donegal.

http://www.dingle-peninsula.ie
Here you can pay a virtual visit to the Gaeltacht area of Corca Dhuibhne in Kerry. You won't need Irish, but the language will be there for you to see being used. (You

can do an on-line search for other Gaeltacht area web sites too.)

http://www.smo.uhi.ac.uk/liosta/
At this site you can sign on to email lists like the Gaelic-B, where learners can share problems and information or ask questions, and help is extended by advanced students and fluent speakers.

http://www.fainne.org/
This is the main page of the Irish language web ring, An Fáinne Órga, which lists and offers connections to many web pages written strictly in Irish. From any of the member sites you can also travel in a circle round the entire ring. Its name, An Fáinne Órga, refers to the gold circle that people sometimes wear to show that they speak Irish.

http://www.artscouncil.ie/index.html
An Chomhairle Ealaíon (The Arts Council)

http://www.filmboard.ie/
Bord Scannán na hÉireann (The Irish Film Board)

http://www.smo.uhi.ac.uk/gaeilge/gaeilge.html
This page lists a few hundred Irish-language related sites. Knowing some Irish will help in moving around the site, but a small amount of English is also given and is helpful to beginners. The sites to which it links are both in English and in Irish, and it is well worth exploring.

http://www.rnag.ie
Raidió na Gaeltachta (RnaG), the Irish-language radio station. You can listen to a live stream of the daily broadcast across the Internet. Programme schedules are provided here too.

http://www.rte.ie/
Raidió Teilifís Éireann (RTÉ) has established an archive page of RnaG programmes, so you can listen to them when the station is off the air or catch a programme you missed. Click on 'Audio Downloads'. You can pick up the RnaG live stream at this site, as well.

http://www.iol.ie/~rnl102/
Raidió na Life. This site contains programme schedules and information, and you can contact the station by email.

http://www.bbc.co.uk/northernireland/blas/
An Irish language programme, Blas, can be heard live over the Internet each evening from Monday to Thursday, 19:30–20:00 GMT. A recording is also made available to listen to the programme on demand.

http://www.tg4.ie/
Teilifís na Gaeilge (TnaG), renamed TG4. Get schedules and read about the shows, even submit your opinion on each programme. The initial site encountered is all in Irish. If you don't have Irish, click on *'In English'* for the English language version.

http://www.rte.ie/aertel/aertelplus/P480.HTM
RTÉ's Aertel service, providing up-to-date information
on what's happening in the Irish language scene.

http://www.nuacht.com/
The web site of the Irish language newspaper *Lá.*

http://www.foinse.ie/
The web site of the Irish language newspaper *Foinse.*

http://www.ireland.com/gaeilge/teangabeo/
An Teanga Bheo. The Irish language portion of the
Irish Times newspaper, published weekly online.

http://www.beo.ie/
Beo. A monthly Internet magazine for Irish speakers in
Ireland and worldwide. *Beo* contains interesting articles
on a wide variety of topics, as well as a special section of
material for learners. To help learners read the articles,
not only are glossaries provided, but the meanings of
certain highlighted phrases are revealed if one's cursor is
placed over them.

IRISH ABROAD

While the history of Irish in Ireland has been thoroughly
researched, not very much is known about the Irish language
in other parts of the world. Of that, more is known about
Old and Middle Irish on the European continent in the
Middle Ages than is known about the course of Modern Irish
that was carried by the millions of emigrants who left Ireland

and were dispersed around the world during the last three hundred years.

When a comprehensive history of Irish worldwide is written, it will show the Irish language experience of the scholars, clergy, merchants and soldiers who journeyed to and from the continent of Europe from earliest times until the seventeenth century. It will talk about the Irish-speaking emigrants to Great Britain, Australia and America from the eighteenth century onwards. And from the end of the nineteenth century to the present, it will follow the progress of the descendants of those emigrants, in all those places, documenting their participation in the movement to restore Irish and to reclaim what their ancestors had cast aside.

During the twentieth century, the history will show that individuals and small groups throughout the world continued the study of Irish, usually in isolation, with whatever teaching resources were available – until the eighties, when colleges and universities around the world began to offer courses in Irish in response to student demand. The history will end at the beginning of a new century and a new millennium, with the Internet making a virtual *Gaeltacht* of the whole world.

5 THE LANGUAGE ITSELF

SOME NOTES ON PRONUNCIATION AND GRAMMAR

This guide will highlight some of differences between Irish and English grammar. The rules of Irish grammar are covered in detail in *Learning Irish* by Micheál Ó Siadhail. *Irish on Your Own* by Éamonn Ó Dónaill and Deirbhle Ní Churraighín has a 23-page section called 'How the Language Works' that is very clear and well organised, and is probably the most painless introduction for beginners. *Teach Yourself Irish* by Diarmaid Ó Sé and Joseph Shiels also covers grammar quite thoroughly. *Beginners' Irish* by Gabriel Rosenstock is good because it does not overwhelm the beginner. Two really useful reference books are *Verbs Regular and Irregular* by Pól Ó Murchú and the *New Irish Grammar* by The Christian Brothers, a compact book containing all the rules. A selection of texts, including those just mentioned, is reviewed in a later section of this chapter, 'Texts for Learning Irish', page 105.

Pronouncing Words

Ideally you will be able to listen to Irish speakers and mimic what they say. If that's not possible, do the same with any of the available learner's tapes. Books that make use of the International Phonetic Alphabet are also helpful. Examples of pronunciation given below are merely approximate.

Broad and slender consonants. Each consonant is pronounced two slightly different ways, depending on whether it is closest to the vowels a, o and u (broad) or e and i (slender). A most noticeable distinction is heard between broad and slender s. A broad s is much like an English s: *solas* (light) is pronounced sull-us. But as you might guess from names like *Sinéad* and *Seán,* a slender s is pronounced like an English sh.

C and g are pronounced with a hard sound in Irish.

Ng is commonly seen at the beginning of words. It is pronounced as in the English word sung.

Long and short vowels. A vowel is short unless it has an accent or length mark (*síneadh fada*). Not alone does the *síneadh fada* change how the word is pronounced, it also changes the meaning of the word. *Cead* (pronounced a bit like 'cad' in English) means 'permission'. *Céad* (pronounced cayd) means 'hundred'.

The neutral vowel sound. This is a sound inserted between l, n, or r, and some other consonants when they directly follow these letters. Some examples are: *bolb* (caterpillar) pronounced as bol-ub; *ainm* (name), as an-im; and *dorcha* (dark) as dor-uh-khuh.

Words ending in 'e'. Unlike English, a final e is always pronounced. In the phrase *éirí na gréine* (sunrise), *gréine* is pronounced greí-neh.

Word Order

In English the order is subject, verb, object, and adjectives precede nouns. The order in an Irish sentence is verb, subject, object. Adjectives follow nouns, as in the following example:

Shiela saw the big ship.

Chonaic Síle an long mhór (Lit. saw Shiela the ship big).

Nouns

Nouns in Irish are either masculine or feminine, and Irish-English dictionaries will indicate that fact. They are divided into five declensions. A knowledge of these elements is necessary in order to use Irish correctly.

Nouns also change to reflect usage of case. Below are some examples of the nominative and genitive cases, using *capall* (horse), a masculine noun:

Nominative, singular:
itheann an capall féar 'the horse eats grass'

Nominative, plural:
itheann na capaill féar 'the horses eat grass'

Genitive, singular: *crúba an chapaill* 'the horse's hooves'

Genitive, plural: *crúba na gcapall* 'the horses' hooves'

In addition to indicating possession, the genitive case in Irish is used after the verbal noun: *Bhí na páistí ag imirt leadóige.* The children were playing tennis (at playing of tennis). It is also used after some prepositions: *i rith an lae,* 'during the day' (in the course of the day).

Adjectives

Usually adjectives add an a in the plural:

gúna bán 'a white dress'
gúnaí bána 'white dresses'

To indicate comparative, usually an e is added, and the final consonant is made slender by preceding it with an i:

Tá an gúna seo níos báine *ná an ceann eile.*
'This dress is *whiter* (more white) than the other one.'

Mutations

In Irish there are two changes, or mutations, undergone by consonants in certain circumstances. One is called *séimhiú* (lenition) and the other is *urú* (eclipsis). *Séimhiú* can occur at the beginning of and within words. It is used to signal the required pronunciation of the affected consonant, which in turn conveys the meaning of the word. *Urú* appears only at the start of words. This, too, affects pronunciation and conveys meaning.

Séimhiú (Lenition)

In Roman style lettering (commonly used since the 1950s), *séimhiú* is indicated by an h following a consonant: *máthair* 'a mother'; *a mháthair* 'his mother'; *a máthair* 'her mother'. Here the lenition at the beginning indicates that the mother is 'his'. (Note that 'her mother' is not lenited.) Irish style lettering, in which *séimhiú* is indicated by a dot over the affected consonant, reveals that the internal 't' also takes a *séimhiú:* ᴀ ṁᴀᴄᴀıɼ 'his mother'. (Without the *séimhiú* dot, or the added 'h' in Roman lettering, the 't' would have a hard sound, rendering this particular word meaningless.)

Urú (Eclipsis)

Urú is achieved by placing a new consonant before what was up until then the first one, and thereby eclipsing it: *pictiúr* 'a picture'; *a bpictiúr* 'their picture'. Certain consonants are used to eclipse specific others and cause them to be pronounced differently.

Verbs

Although most Irish verbs are regular, the eleven irregular verbs are among those most widely used in daily speech, so they must be mastered early in the learning process. There are five tenses in Irish, plus subjunctive and imperative.

As in many languages, Irish has two verbs to express being; both are irregular. In the following two lines, note that in English 'she is' is the same in both sentences, while in Irish it is quite different:

'She is happy'   and   'She is a beautiful woman'
'Tá *sí sásta*'   but   'Is *bean álainn í*'

Broadly, the first denotes a transitory state of being (happiness), the second an innate quality of the subject (beauty). This is just one simple example of a point of grammar that usually has at least one chapter devoted to it in the learning texts.

While memorising rules of grammar cannot be avoided, modern methods of second language acquisition make the process easier than it was in the 1950s, when *Teach Yourself Irish* by Myles Dillon was the only book available for the adult beginner.

The invasions of Ireland by peoples from other lands contributed to the vocabulary of Irish.

Many Latin words came from neighbouring Wales and other parts of Celtic Britain, which was occupied by the Roman legions for a time. The Latin brought by Christian clerics consists mostly of vocabulary associated with the church, religion and writing:

Irish	Latin	English
eaglais	ecclesia	church
easpag	episcopus	bishop
sagart	sacerdos	priest
leabhar	liber	book
paidir	pater	prayer
scríobh	scribo	write

The Viking incursions of the ninth century brought Scandinavian words, including these:

Irish	Scandinavian	English
pónaire	baunir	bean
seol	segl	sail
bróg	brok	shoe
cnaipe	knappr	button

The Anglo-Normans first became involved in Ireland in the late twelfth century, introducing a large number of words directly – or indirectly through English – from Norman French:

Irish	Norman	English
aturnae	aturnee	attorney
bagún	bacun	bacon
seomra	chambre	chamber, room
mailís	malis	malice

Many words later came from English, but once the language restoration began in the 1890s, hundreds of new terms in Irish were created as needed for the modern age. This creation of necessary terms continues into the present.

TEXTS FOR LEARNING IRISH

Courses in Books, Tapes and CDs

Learning Irish by Micheál Ó Siadhail. A complete course created as a college-level text. This course is suitable for those who are prepared to do intensive study. Speakers on the tape use regional Connemara speech of the Cois Fhairrge district. Book and four tapes. (Book and tapes available separately.)

Now You're Talking (U.S. title: *Irish on Your Own*) by Éamonn Ó Dónaill and Deirbhle Ní Churraighín. A self-guided course. Consists of a book and three cassette tapes. Ulster regional speech throughout. The material is attractively presented in full colour.

Beginners Irish by Gabriel Rosenstock has some unique features, including his emphasis on prepositions, which he calls the 'The Building Blocks of Irish'. He recommends studying them over and over in order to improve one's oral and written Irish and gives a lot of examples. His comments throughout are interesting and helpful.

Buntús Cainte. A beginner's course in spoken Irish. Short simple lessons. The method relies on listening, repeating and constant revision. Rules of grammar are not given. (These can be found in books like the *New Irish Grammar.*) Speakers on the tapes use standard Irish. The course consists of three books and six tapes, available in units of one book and two tapes each.

Irish for Beginners. Twenty lessons are in this brightly illustrated book with tape, which is a favourite for beginner classes. Lessons contain sentences and phrases that can be used daily.

Teach Yourself Irish. There is a new edition of this long-established teaching system, completely revised by Diarmaid Ó Sé and Joseph Sheils. It has two accompanying tapes. Standard Irish.

Abair Leat, Parts I and II. These excellent books by Éamonn Ó Dónaill and Siuán Ní Mhaonaigh fill a long-felt need for teachers who want to improve their own language skills. Both books have accompanying tapes. Éamonn Ó Dónaill is a co-author of the language course *Irish On Your Own.*

Learn Irish Now! This CD-ROM has extensive grammar, learning games and tests, and stories with video clips and illustrations. Listen to soundtracks as you read, or choose to have each word and sentence pronounced separately. Interactive phrases let you record yourself to compare your pronunciation with that of the speaker on the CD. Better for intermediate learners, probably difficult for absolute beginners. Compatible with both Windows and Apple Macintosh.

Learn Irish: Talk Now. CD-ROM. Essential words and phrases for the absolute beginner. It is interactive: compare your pronunciation with that of the speaker on the CD. Monitor your progress. Suitable for Windows and Apple Macintosh.

SpeakWrite Irish. A speech-based computer aid to learning Irish. Interactive speech, instant record and playback, speech speed control, CD-quality sound, extensive grammar reference. Can run on an Apple Macintosh or Windows operating system. IBM compatible. A brochure describes the technical requirements. Has three course units of ten segments each.

Language 30 Irish. Stresses useful words and phrases. Approximately one and a half hours of guided practice in greetings, introductions, asking for things in shops and hotels. Booklet and two tapes. No grammar.

Cogar. A course in conversational Irish, suitable as a supplement to any of the basic courses. Covers the main topics of casual conversation. Lively and amusing; based on the latest theories of language learning. Some of the material was recorded live in Connemara. Four tapes with study notes.

Enough Irish to Get By. Booklet with phrases. Clear standard Irish on the tape.

The Irish Phrasebook / An Ráleabhar Gaeilge by D. Ó Donnchadha. More than 42 subject headings. Useful in a conversation group.

Basic Irish for Parents. This is designed to help parents whose children are attending the all-Irish primary schools in Ireland. Covers the usual parent-child situations. Has an accompanying tape, with choice of standard speech or the regional speech of Munster, Connaught, or Ulster. The tapes are very clear.

Grammars

New Irish Grammar. Standard, concise grammar written in English. An excellent reference text.

Buntús Gramadaí. A basic grammar used in junior schools in Ireland. Irish is used throughout. Practice exercises are given in each chapter. Useful for an advanced beginner class or an intermediate one.

Tús na Gramadaí. An introduction and workbook in 24 lessons. Very clearly laid out, with plenty of exercises for classwork or homework. Combined with *Buntús Cainte,* this would make a good beginner's learning packet for several semesters.

Briathra na Gaeilge by D. & P. Ó Murchú. Lists all tenses for the most commonly used Irish verbs, regular and irregular. Very well organised.

Dictionaries

Beginner's Irish Dictionary. A well-designed, full-colour, English-Irish pictorial dictionary arranged according to themes, so that it can be easily used in conversation. The reader can see at a glance the basic vocabulary for such things as holidays, driving, shopping, work and ninety other topics. Contains a simple guide to Irish grammar. Very good for a beginning conversation class.

Foclóir Póca. Irish-English/English-Irish pocket dictionary with over 30,000 words, a pronunciation guide using international phonetic symbols, new terminology, and a short explanation of some aspects of Irish grammar, with verb tables.

Foclóir Póca Learner's Cassette. Comes with accompanying explanatory booklet, which illustrates how to pronounce Irish according to the sound system used in the pocket dictionary above.

Foclóir Gaeilge-Béarla. Compiled by Niall Ó Dónaill. Standard unabridged modern Irish-English dictionary. This 1,200-page work is essential for writers because it gives so many examples of usage.

Irish-English / English-Irish Dictionary (for computer) by Niall Ó Dónaill. This two-way version of the above dictionary is not available in hard copy. Windows compatible.

English-Irish Dictionary. Compiled by Tomás de Bhaldraithe. Complete, unabridged. It is the standard English-Irish dictionary.

The Irish Language by Máirtín Ó Murchú. The author is one of the foremost scholars in Irish language and linguistics studies.

Irish Language Ireland. Fact Pack / Ireland Guides. This is a 36-page pocket booklet with concise entries on many aspects of Irish-language Ireland. It gives names, addresses, phone numbers and brief descriptions of schools, government agencies, festivals, newspapers and places of interest. In addition, it includes a wonderful fold-out map of each Irish-speaking region. People who want to access Irish-language Ireland will find this book really useful. It is one of a series on aspects of Irish culture published by Morrigan Books.

An Ghaeilge, a haghaidh roimpi / Irish, Facing the Future. Prepared by Helen Ó Murchú, former President of the European Bureau for Lesser Used Languages, and published by the Irish Committee of this organisation. This book presents the most definitive information on the present state of the language. It begins with an essay on the course of the language from earliest times to the present by Máirtín Ó Murchú. Next are results and analyses of the most recent census and surveys. The chapter 'Constitutional, Legal, and Administrative Provision for Irish' presents a concise summary of eighty years of Government policy and action for the language. The other sections are on the status of the language in education, the arts and economic life. The material on the status of Irish in the north was supplied by Aodán Mac Póilin. There is an extraordinary amount of information in this book, presenting a realistic picture of Irish today. It will probably have far-reaching effects on language policy for the future and will be invaluable for teachers, students and people engaged in language planning. The book is bilingual.

The Oxford Companion to Irish Literature edited by Robert Welch. At least forty Irish-language scholars contributed to this useful reference work, which has essays on major topics and shorter entries on individual writers from earliest times to the present. It is cross-referenced throughout with a chronology and maps, and is especially valuable on the writings of medieval Ireland.

A Dictionary of Anglo-Irish Words and Phrases from Gaelic in the English of Ireland by Diarmuid Ó Muirithe. Thousands of words and phrases collected and presented to show the extent to which Irish enriches daily English speech in Ireland.

NEWSPAPERS AND PERIODICALS

Foinse. An Cheathrú Rua, Co. na Gaillimhe (County Galway), http://www.foinse.ie/, a national newspaper published weekly on Sundays.

Lá. 301 Bóthar an Ghleanna, Béal Feirste (Belfast), http://www.nuacht.com/, a national weekly newspaper on sale each Thursday.

Comhar. Comhar Teo., 5 Cearnóg Mhuirfean, Baile Átha Cliath 2, a monthly arts, literature and current affairs magazine.

Saol. 7 Cearnóg Mhuirfean (Merrion Row), Baile Átha Cliath 2 (Dublin), http://www.smo.uhi.ac.uk/gaeilge/ saol.html, a monthly publication on events in the Irish language community.

Feasta. An Siopa Leabhar, 6 Sráid Fhearchair, Baile Átha Cliath 2, a monthly magazine.

In addition, many English language newspapers publish columns in Irish regularly, such as the *Irish Times, Irish News, Glór Chonamara, Andersonstown News, Irish Echo* (US) and the *Irish Herald* (US).

SUMMER SCHOOLS

Below are some of the organisations that were offering summer courses in Irish for adults as of 2001:

East (Leinster):

Áras Uí Ghramhnaigh, Ráth Cairn, Co. na Mí
(County Meath), Éire.
Tel. (046) 32067,
http://www.rathcairn.com/

South West (Munster):

Oidhreacht Chorca Dhuibhne, Baile an Fheirtéaraigh,
Trá Lí, Co. Chiarraí (County Kerry), Éire.
Tel.(066) 56100,
http://www.corca-dhuibhne.com/oidhreacht.html

West (Connaught):

Áras Mháirtín Uí Chadhain, An Cheathrú Rua, Co. na Gaillimhe (County Galway), Éire. This centre is part of the Department of Irish of University College, Galway. Both college credit and non-credit courses are offered. Tel. (091) 95101, http://www.mis.ucg.ie/International_Office/ Summer_School/IrishLanguage.html

North West (Ulster):

Oideas Gael, Gleann Cholm Cille, Co. Dhún na nGall (County Donegal), Éire. Tel. (073) 30248 or (073) 30348, http://www.oideas-gael.com

An Chrannóg, Srath na Corcra, Na Doirí Beaga, Leitir Ceanainn, Tír Chonaill (County Donegal), Éire. Tel. (075) 32188, http://members.nbci.com/crannog/

Dáil Uladh, Comhchoiste na Gaeilge. Teach an Cheoil, Bóthar an Droichid, Dún Lathaí, Co. Aontroma (County Antrim), BT44 9AN, N. Ireland. (Courses are held in the Gort an Choirce Gaeltacht in Co. Donegal.) Tel. (012656) 57096, http://www.gaeilge-comhchoiste.com/

Foras na Gaeilge

The body responsible for all-island promotion of the Irish language. The responsibilities and staff of Bord na Gaeilge, An Gúm (publishers) and An Coiste Téarmaíochta (terminology development) have all been transferred here. They are happy to provide information upon request on what is available in the way of places to learn, read, hear and use the Irish language.

> 7 Cearnóg Mhuirfean (7 Merrion Square),
> Baile Átha Cliath 2 (Dublin 2)
> Tel. 01 639 8400, email: eolas@forasnagaeilge.ie,
> web: http://www.forasnagaeilge.ie

Comhdháil Náisiúnta na Gaeilge

Central-Council for the Irish speaking community, acting as a forum for Irish Language organisations and other related groups. Provides information on any aspect of using Irish in daily life.

> 46 Sráid Chill Dara (46 Kildare Street),
> Baile Átha Cliath 2 (Dublin 2)
> Tel. 01 679 4780, email: eolas@comhdhail.ie, web:
> http://www.comhdhail.ie

An Comhchoiste Réamhscolaíochta

Helps establish and develop *Naíonraí* (Irish language pre-schools). Provides information and advice on using Irish with young children.

7 Cearnóg Mhuirfean (7 Merrion Square),
Baile Átha Cliath 2 (Dublin 2)
Tel. 01 639 8400

Gaelscoileanna

Helps parents find all-Irish education for their children and provides services to all-Irish schools.

7 Cearnóg Mhuirfean (7 Merrion Square),
Baile Átha Cliath 2 (Dublin 2)
Tel. 01 639 8400, email: oifig@gaelscoileanna.iol.ie,
web: http://www.iol.ie/gaelscoileanna/

Gaeloiliúint

Provides support to all-Irish schools in the north of Ireland and helps parents find all-Irish education for their children.

216 Bóthar na bhFál (216 Falls Road),
Béal Feirste BT12 6AH (Belfast BT12 6AH)
Tel. 028 90 247222, email: eolas@gaeloiliuint.ie,
web: http://www.gaeloiliuint.ie

InterCelt

Provides information on Irish language holiday opportunities anywhere in Ireland.

46 Sráid Chill Dara (46 Kildare Street),
Baile Átha Cliath 2 (Dublin 2)
Tel. 01 679 4780, email: eolas@comhdhail.ie,
web: http://www.intercelt.ie

Gaelsaoire

Provides information on Irish language holiday and course opportunities in any of the *Gaeltacht* areas.

> Údarás na Gaeltachta
> Sráid an Dóirin,
> An Daingean (Dingle), Co. Chiarraí (County Kerry)
> Tel. 01 679 4780, email: info@gaelsaoire.ie,
> web: http://www.gaelsaoire.ie

Comhchoiste Náisiúnta na gColáistí Samhraidh (CONCOS)

Provides information on Irish summer colleges for young people (in and outside the *Gaeltachta*).

> Coláiste Chorca Dhuibhne, Baile an Fheirtéirigh,
> Co. Chiarraí (County Kerry)
> Tel. 066 915 6100

Údarás na Gaeltachta

Government agency responsible for economic development in the *Gaeltachtaí,* and for preservation of Irish as the principal language of the Gaeltacht community.

> Na Forbacha,
> Gaillimh (Galway)
> Tel. 091 503100, email: eolas@unagt.ie,
> web: http://www.udaras.ie

Appendix

ON THEIR EXPERIENCES AT SUMMER SCHOOL

There is now a wide choice of Irish-language summer schools for adult learners, with courses lasting from one weekend to six weeks.

Accommodation can be arranged in hotels or in private homes with Irish-speaking families. Most such schools are in the west of the country. An exception is Áras Uí Ghramhnaigh, in Meath, about 40 miles from Dublin (a feature that might be desirable for some travellers).

Each of these schools is unique to its locality, and each reflects the passion for Irish of its founder/director. All are thrilled that people from abroad want to learn Irish and, as the following essays show, the students' enthusiasm is boundless. They are all written by Americans who travelled to Ireland to attend summer courses.

Learning Irish

at Áras Mháirtín Uí Chadhain

by Barbara Thompson

My great-great grandfather left County Sligo for America in 1795. He died on his way to Indiana, but his widow homesteaded what is now the O'Hara family farm there. Because of this I have always been interested in all things Irish, but what I learned was mostly through books. I had long felt a need for help in pronouncing the beautiful names of Irish places and people, and when I happened on a course in Irish being taught at the University of Arizona I enrolled immediately. After a year of attending classes for two hours a week and studying from two to six hours a day, I decided that a brief intensive course would help my conversational skills.

Because it suited my time schedule and that of my friend Áine, I chose a two-week course in Ireland at Áras Mháirtin Uí Chadhain. For learning Irish in a stimulating environment or to brush up one's skills and have fun at the same time, there is no better choice than this, the Irish language center of University College, Galway, in An Cheathrú Rua, Connemara.

The bus ride from Galway City to An Cheathrú Rua (Carraroe in English) took about two hours. The *bean an tí* (woman of the house or landlady) met us at the bus stop and soon we were at "home," where we met Pól and Páraicín from Melbourne, Australia, who would be our fellow students for the next two weeks; the fifth student would meet us at the school the next morning.

The house we stayed in was comfortable. All the rooms had large windows that overlooked a pretty lawn with flowers and a lake or inlet at the back. The decor was simple but pleasant. We were invited to make use of the living room and we spent time there watching Irish television, reading, studying, visiting, and talking with the bean an tí when she had time to spare from meal preparation. I cannot express in words how wonderful the food was; every meal was delicious and beautifully presented. We were not surprised to learn that our *bean an tí* teaches cooking classes and had been a chef.

Pól and Páraicín told us they had been studying Irish on and off for about twelve years. Pól works in administration with the postal service in Australia and Páraicín teaches Japanese at the University in Melbourne. Our fifth student was from Germany. She teaches at the University in Galway and decided that after living in Ireland for nine years it was time to learn the native language. Our teacher, Nuala, quickly made us feel at ease and was enthusiastic about teaching us. When she found out our varying levels of Irish, she quickly adjusted her lesson plans to accommodate us.

There was another group of fourteen students there for a

one-week advanced course. We shared coffee breaks (which we soon learned to call *"sos"*) with these fluent speakers. It was a challenge following their involved conversations, but they were generous in their efforts to help. One of them was from Colorado, another from Italy, and the rest were Irish.

The class was interesting even as we started with *tá sé fuar inniu* (it is cold today) and worked our way diligently through the course. We finished on schedule, including a brief journey into the murky waters of the future tense. Áine and I covered more material in the two weeks at *"Áras"* than we did in six months in Arizona. Of course, we had more than twenty minutes a week to practice speaking in class and we had people to speak Irish with every waking moment if we chose. We were also able to ask questions, which there is not time for in Arizona. Our teacher was full of questions and used them to get us talking to her and each other. Each morning she asked us in Irish what was new and we told her what we had for breakfast, lunch, supper, where we had gone, what we had seen, whether we had been to the pub, when we got home, and what time we went to bed. We played guessing games as to the ownership of pens, pencils, bags, coats, etc. Naturally, we did the well-prepared hand-outs and checked our homework. The second week, the teacher innocently said that we might ask her questions. We had been hoping for that and got out the sheets of questions we had prepared over the weekend. She was a good sport and answered our questions as to what she had done on Saturday night, with whom, where, how long, etc. We had a lot of fun teasing her (all in Irish of course).

Our printed class schedule was in English the first week, but the second week it was in Irish. All the signs posted around the school were in Irish and we found it necessary to carry our pocket dictionaries. At meals the radio was tuned to the news and other programs in Irish. By the second week, I was able to understand more than the very simple words. Our *bean an tí* spoke to us in Irish, but would translate if necessary. She was a rich source for new vocabulary.

Breandán Ó Hara took over the class from 4:00 to 5:00 pm. In his class we watched videos and listened to tapes of fairy tales. We played a version of "twenty questions," and that is harder than it sounds when it is all done in Irish. We had exercises on colors, time, numbers, and the thirty-two counties of Ireland. Breandán also teaches at University College, Galway.

Seán Ó Flatharta took us on a tour to the small islands near An Cheathrú Rua, stopping often so that we could photograph the wild flowers, the swans, and the rocks (always the rocks).

One evening there was Irish dancing and another evening we gathered to hear Máire Uí Dhroighneáin sing. She has a beautiful voice and sang for an hour. Then we joined her in singing "Cúnnla," "An Cailín Álainn," and "Cóilin Phádraic Sheámais."

The following week we plowed ahead with the language and had more singing and dancing. The advanced class had departed, and the school and village were flooded with young people. They, too, were far advanced in speaking Irish, but thought our American accents in Irish were "cool."

By the end of the week the bad weather had cleared so that it was safe for our class to go on an outing to one of the Aran Islands, which are situated about thirty miles southwest of Galway. The ferry ride to Inishmaan, the middle island in location and size, took about two hours; our teacher accompanied us. We were met at the dock by our guide, Máirín Ní Chonghaile, a life-time resident of Inishmaan. She is a widow and has two daughters, with whom she speaks only Irish. After tea and homemade scones in front of a turf fire, Máirín took us on a tour of the island. We walked quickly, as Máirín had many things to show us before the ferry returned to take us home. Máirín spoke only in Irish and did not hesitate to correct our grammar or pronunciation. We loved it.

The view of the island and of the Atlantic was breathtaking. We stopped at the cottage once occupied by the dramatist John Millington Synge. It was Máirín's home when she was growing up. Her sister, who now owns it, is restoring it and will open a tea shop there next year.

This was our last adventure. It was with heavy hearts that we said good-bye to our teacher and our classmates and friends at the Áras.

There will be a course for students at the intermediate level for four weeks next summer. Áine and I talk of taking it, but we have been told the schedule is brutal (more than eight hours of classes a day, including two and one-half hours in the evenings). The alternative is to repeat the beginning class. Whichever we take, I am sure we will both go back to Ireland next year.

Learning Irish at An Chrannóg

by Duane H. Farabaugh

I began actively studying the Irish language in 1989 as a junior in high school. The reasons for embarking on this seemingly esoteric pursuit for an American were many. In exploring Irish roots on my mother's side, I found I have great-grandparents who came from areas of Limerick and Kerry that were still Irish-speaking when they emigrated. Being detached from the immigrant generation, I had little contact with Ireland or Irish culture growing up. I was always told that the Gaelic language was extinct – that it was completely wiped out in the Famine, a misconception that many Americans of Irish descent share.

In discovering that the language indeed still survived as a daily spoken language in the *Gaeltachtaí,* and that Irish was a required subject in all Irish schools, I decided to connect with this severed linguistic and cultural tie. Being very curious about languages in general – at the time I was dabbling in Chinese – I got the book *Teach Yourself Irish* and began tackling the exercises. Then I discovered that weekly Irish classes were being offered at the Ancient Order of Hibernians in the nearby town of Babylon, Long Island, which I soon began attending. Next, I found Séamus Blake's Irish-language radio program, *"Míle Fáilte,"* on Saturday mornings, which I diligently listened to and taped. Gradually, I acquired the basic grammar of the language and was able to speak in simple sentences.

While at Binghamton University I majored in German. The enthusiasm of the late Professor Larry Wells for German language and culture and his tremendous language-teaching ability spurred on a similar enthusiasm in myself. I took advantage of the two study-abroad programs offered by the university, one in Graz, Austria, and the other at the University of Leipzig, Germany. Following graduation, I spent a year in Austria as a teaching assistant at a high school in the town of Jennersdorf, near the Hungarian border. During this time it was difficult to continue with Irish, although I worked on maintaining what I had learned through books and tapes. I also tried to seek out people at Binghamton and in Austria and Germany (or wherever I happened to be) who spoke Irish, and we would exchange simple phrases.

In 1996, while working in New York City, I began taking classes at Ireland House, New York University, with Pádraig Ó Cearúil, and since then my ability to communicate in Irish has improved dramatically. For me, Pádraig is to Irish what Larry Wells was to German, a master language teacher. Pádraig is a native speaker from Gaoth Dobhair, in northwest Donegal. The music groups Clannad and Altan and the singer

Enya all come from this region. It also has An Chrannóg, a center for promoting the culture and language of the area, and I decided to attend a summer immersion course in Irish there.

I traveled by bus from Shannon Airport to Gaoth Dobhair, via Galway. I was able to start practising Irish straight away with a man sitting beside me. He was a police officer from Letterkenny, the main town in Donegal, and spoke Irish fluently. I had noticed he had been talking to the bus driver, who I knew was an Irish speaker. I asked him why he had spoken in English to the bus driver, when they could have just as easily conversed in Irish. He couldn't really give me a good answer. He was surprised as to my motives for learning Irish and asked repeatedly if I was involved with the IRA. He seemed baffled that an American would be speaking Irish. Otherwise we had a good conversation.

I chatted in Irish with one of the bus workers, who was from the Gaoth Dobhair region himself, and I was relieved to find I had little problem understanding him. Arriving at An Chrannóg, Pádraig Mac Con Uladh met me and addressed me in rapid-fire Irish. I told him I had made arrangements to stay at the *Bia agus Leaba* (Bed and Breakfast) of Áine Ní Rortaigh.

Linguistically, the family I stayed with was certainly purely Irish speaking, but I immediately discovered that this dialect was a struggle to understand (of course). The radio in the kitchen was tuned to Raidió na Gaeltachta during the entire day, the reception of which was crystal clear (the broadcasting station is two blocks away). I felt the children of the house a bit apprehensive about speaking Irish with me, but I was able to hold my own in the conversations I did have with them, and for the most part I resisted the temptation to speak English. When the family conversed among themselves, it was difficult to follow. The dialect would take some getting used to. The Ulster dialect of Irish reminds me a lot of the Austrian dialect of German compared to the High German that is considered standard. Ulster Irish as heard in Gaoth Dobhair sounds just very different from what I learned in the United States.

In addition to the lodging, breakfast and dinner were included in the price of £20 a day, plus tea-time cookies and sandwiches. The food, incidentally, was excellent, especially the Irish breakfast. The potatoes were particularly delectable.

The course at An Chrannóg was certainly worth the price of £110. It consisted of two daily sessions with each of the two teachers, Pádraig Ó Cearúil and Pádraig Mac Con Uladh, from 9:30 to 11:15 am. and from 12:00 to 1:45 PM. Pádraig Mac Con Uladh's aggressive style of very direct immersion – speaking extensively in high speed Irish – contrasts strongly with Pádraig Ó Cearúil's calmer, more methodical approach, which focuses on having students do most of the speaking. Besides myself, there were four women in the class: one from London (originally from County Armagh), one from Fermanagh who teaches at an Irish-medium nursery school, a recent college graduate from Letterkenny, and another woman from England who had been living in Gaoth Dobhair for nine months and was involved in acquiring a Celtic Studies degree. In comparison with theirs, I felt that my Irish was at a lower tier, as all the others generally had had several years of formal Irish instruction and had spent more time in Gaeltacht areas. But this pressure helped me rise to a higher level.

After the second session each day, field trips were planned. These provided a great opportunity to speak Irish in a natural social atmosphere, although accompanied by the teachers who were there to correct any grammatical difficulties. The first trip, on Monday, was a walk over to the beach where Pádraig Ó Cearúil discussed vocabulary dealing with special features of the coast land. Another trip was to the childhood home of Micí Mac Gabhann, a Gaoth Dobhair native who made a fortune in the Klondike gold rush and then came back to live in the area in his old age. A girl of maybe sixteen or seventeen gave us a tour of the three-room house. Amazingly, her dialect of Irish differed markedly from the variety that was spoken fourteen miles down the road. It had much more of a drawl to it. After a short tour we saw a documentary film about Micí Mac Gabhann.

We visited several other well-known sites in the area. We visited the Poison Glen – or the Holy Glen, depending on whether you say *Gleann Nimhe* or *Gleann Naofa* – now Glenveagh National Park, which was once the estate of a British landlord. During the bus trip Pádraig Mac Con Uladh was chatting with the driver in Irish. There were also hiking trails leading up several hills around the area, from which I caught some magnificent views of the vast, barren landscapes of central Donegal.

The night life in Gaoth Dobhair was certainly alive. I went to several of the pubs in the area, and there was live music every night. I conversed for the most part in Irish, and discovered there were a great number of visitors like myself there to improve their Irish, mainly from the six counties and particularly from Belfast and Derry. There were also a number of other Europeans, Germans and French, either working at the nearby factories or vacationing there. My first night in Gaoth Dobhair I went to the famous Leo's Tavern, where I saw Leo himself luring patrons to sing along with him, "You've heard of Karaoke, well here we have Leo-oke!" They also had a disco that night at Óstán Radharc na Mara. For some reason I didn't expect such a disco in the middle of the Gaeltacht. There was quite a crowd there, it resembled the dance club I had been to in Galway the night before. I chatted with two fifteen-year-old girls outside as it was closing up around three in the morning. I was speaking with them in Irish, and soon I found out that one of them was from Germany, but was living in the area because her father was a manager at a local factory. To my surprise, the Irish girl spoke German as well, and also French. German she had learned through her friend, and French she had learned in school. Quadrilingual at 15 without leaving Gaoth Dobhair. That impressed me.

I met several other interesting people during my stay. I made the acquaintance of a very lovely French mademoiselle from the Pyrenees, with whom I went out a few times. She was working as an accounting intern at a local factory for the summer. I also met a free lance journalist from New York who had been living in Gaoth Dobhair for over a year and whose articles about the area had appeared in the *New York Times*. At a *céilí* at Teach Jack several young step-dancers put on a breathtaking display of talent, rivaling those who perform in Riverdance. There was also a *seisiún* at An Chrannóg one night, where there were a few *sean-nós* singers who were phenomenal.

I would certainly highly recommend the An Chrannóg program, but only to those who already have basic conversational ability in Irish, although classes for beginners may have been added since I was there.

On the way back to Shannon airport I spent a night in Galway city and tried to use my Irish. At a chic Italian restaurant I spoke only Irish with the waitress, who willingly answered in Irish, although somewhat bemusedly. It was my general experience, however, that people in Galway city would simply answer in English when addressed in Irish.

My last day in Ireland, I decided to take a trip to the Aran Islands. On the bus to Rossaveal, where the ferry to Inis Mór disembarks, a woman seated next to me happened to be a native Aran Islander. I was able to converse with her in Irish with little difficulty. Upon arrival at Kilronan, the major town on Inis Mór, I rented a bicycle, the standard way to see the island. I spoke Irish to all the local people I met including children. At the far end of the island an elderly man of whom I asked directions was surprised when I told him I was an American, and I felt linguistically that this was a compliment. Cycling round the island I bumped into the woman with whom I had shared the bus ride. She happened to live in the house directly across the way, and invited me in for tea. Inis Mór is really a small world.

Although my time in the Irish-speaking parts of Ireland was only ten days, my Irish improved greatly. I picked up new vocabulary, phrases, and idioms and grew more comfortable with conversational Irish. I look forward to returning to Gaoth Dobhair, and hope to stay much longer – maybe even several months.

A Summer Course in
Baile An Fheirtéaraigh (Ballyferriter)

by Margaret-Mary Connevey

Irish is not a language needed for survival or prosperity in my world, but my desire to learn it was strong. I chose to study in Ballyferriter, on Kerry's Dingle Peninsula, because my mother's parents had come from Listowel and Ballybunion in North Kerry, not too far from there.

Before we left home we had received detailed information about transportation and lodging. At the bus station in Dingle we were met by Máire Uí Shítigh (pronounced "ee heetig"). She was the person in charge of our education for the next two weeks, the person who (we were to become convinced) could solve any problem. After a warm welcome at our Irish-speaking B&B, we had time to settle in and look around.

Four courses were offered: Beginners, Post-Beginners, Conversation, and Language and Heritage. Our reservation form, instead of asking how long we had studied Irish (an embarrassing question for some of us), asked us instead to choose which of five descriptions best fit our level of proficiency:

Never studied Irish
Have some words and phrases
Can understand, but cannot converse
Can converse for 10 minutes
Spoken Irish is fluent, but grammar is poor

Most of us could walk to school in ten or twenty minutes along a road bordered by hedges of fuchsia and wildflowers. Behind them were cattle grazing in green fields between the road and the sea. We passed houses with neat gardens whose flowers had obviously enjoyed the long hours of daylight and the "rainiest summer in thirty years." Next came the church, the pub, the post office, the Museum-Café, the supermarket, and the local school, our school.

Once in that school, we worked on conversation, grammar and vocabulary. We learned and laughed, and learned some more. The teacher, a native speaker from the area, was very patient, making sure that each person spoke, and that all our questions were answered. He often came with us when we took a break for tea or for lunch at the Museum-Café, which was affiliated with our school, but was also open to the public.

The Museum-Café was a popular place for several reasons. In the café the food was tasty, nicely prepared, and varied. We could buy books and tapes about the language and the Irish-speaking area of which Baile an Fheirtéaraigh is a part. In the museum we could get a quick education on the surrounding locality. The friendly staff encouraged us to try out our newly-learned phrases on them before we did so in town. Gradually it got easier.

Although we worked hard in class, that is not all that took place. Local people came to speak to us. They showed slides and movies, and shared with us their music, poetry, and some not-impossible dance steps. In the pubs, we could get a good solid meal and, sometimes, music. One night, we went to a cabaret in a hotel in Dingle. Another day, we went to the Great Blasket Centre to learn about the way of life of the hard-working inhabitants of the Blasket Islands. It has been said that no other community of such small size has ever produced such a wealth of great literature. The people were removed from the islands in 1953.

History was all around us. On one of our field trips, we visited a few of the 2,000 archeological sites found on this small scenic peninsula. Imagine the variety: Megalithic remains (1500 BC), "beehive" houses and Ogham stones (1500 BC to AD 400), Christian sites such as Riasc (c. 5th century AD), and Gallaras Oratory (c. 9th century AD). Near to these are forts and monasteries ruined by the more recent invaders.

The past, the present, the language, and the laughter were as one entity – a richness to be savored and remembered.

Ríocht Na Gréine, or,

Chasing a Dream

(Oideas Gael)

by Séamas Ó Feinneadh

I firmly believe that I was fated to learn Irish! I also feel a strong obligation towards those of my ancestors who may have emigrated from Ireland to the United States in the last century, losing their native language along the way. These two strands of my story, fate and duty, have propelled me over the past 20-odd years to pursue a dream, which, until very recently, when I was finally able to visit Ireland and see for myself, I was not sure had any basis in reality. My bittersweet search for Irish in Ireland did not fully satisfy my craving to immerse myself in the language of my forefathers, but it did reinforce my desire to continue what I have often felt has been a self-induced one-man campaign to ensure that the language will continue to live on through me in my small corner of the world!

The story of what began as idle curiosity, turned into a

strong interest, and finally developed into what some might term an outright obsession, began in 1976 with a little blue book called *Ríocht na Gréine.*

I discovered this slim volume of poetry in a second-hand bookstore in Washington, DC, and although I had never seen this language in print before, I knew instinctively that it must be Irish. I was curious, and was determined to discover the meaning of the title and as much about what this book contained as I possibly could. I also wanted to know something about its editor, Séamas Ó Céilleachair, whose signed photograph appeared on the frontispiece. This led to the purchase of *Teach Yourself Irish,* which many will recall was one of a series originally published with a bright yellow cover, purporting to enable the layman to learn a difficult subject on his own. Actually, however, the original version of this textbook, which has now been completely updated and revised, was so difficult that it challenged me even more to plunge ahead and learn this strange-looking language that I had never heard anyone speak. The next step was the Conversaphone record, a popular series of language-learning LPs. Strangely enough, even before listening to the record the first time, I knew what Irish would sound like and, indeed, the minute I heard the first sounds from the voice on the record, I felt again as if I was already familiar in some way with this language that I was not even sure was still alive in the country where it had originated!

This "voyage of discovery" began slowly at first, for I was basically learning Irish in a complete vacuum. I felt like a detective following leads. Not knowing how else to proceed, I wrote to the publisher of my little blue book, and received a catalogue in return. This led to the discovery of the Irish

Government publishing branch, An Gúm, an employee of which answered my questions about ordering books in a charming letter *as Gaeilge,* and encouraged me to continue my studies. This personal interest on the part of someone I had never met before has been a recurring experience in my acquisition of Irish, and has encouraged me to forge ahead. Unfortunately, however, when I tried another enquiry many years later, the personal touch at An Gúm had been replaced by the personal computer, and I was just another invoice number!

The search for the meaning of *Ríocht na Gréine* has taken me, in my armchair, all over Ireland, and that first, strange little book has now been joined by over 300 others. (I wish I could have everything ever published in Irish!) With no Internet back then, I could not, with just the click of a mouse, find the answers to all my questions about Irish so easily. I subscribed to magazines such as *Comhar* and *Feasta,* and felt as though I would be letting the language down if I did not contribute to the "language movement" by receiving an Irish-language newspaper each week. When I discovered what a precarious state Irish was in, something in me must have decided that I would not be the one to let it die, and that if the last native speaker disappeared, and no one published a single word in Irish ever again, I, at least, would have a repository in my house of what had been the proud expression of a people's hopes and aspirations for many centuries! This is admittedly an extremely naive and romantic approach to language learning, but when fate and duty are the motivating factors, all other considerations fall by the wayside!

Why I did not travel to Ireland until just recently to observe the situation with my own eyes, and to hear with my own ears Irish being spoken by native speakers, may have been ascribable to the fact that I was afraid of what I would find (no one speaking Irish anywhere!); perhaps I felt safer protecting my store of books and tapes for posterity than having to deal with the reality of the Irish language in Ireland today. Who knows? But while I was indeed disappointed that even in the *Gaeltacht* areas more English seems to be present than 'Irish, I was also encouraged by the fact that many are doing so much to promote the language. I could thus return home confidently and continue my campaign in my "*Gaeltacht* of one" to ensure that I do my share to safeguard the legacy of my ancestors!

To remove all doubt that fate was behind my finding that little blue book of poetry, imagine the thrill I felt many years later in my job as a translator for the US Government when, on the occasion of President Reagan's visit to Ireland, a letter arrived for him in Irish that I was privileged to translate, and that letter – call it coincidence, but I call it fate – was from none other than Séamas Ó Céilleachair! I could not help but feel that the editor of *Ríocht na Gréine* must have known that his message would be conveyed to the President by someone who had been preparing for that moment ever since his eyes fell on that small book of verse *fadó, fadó*. Indeed, I have finally learned the meaning of those magical words in the title, taken from a beautiful poem in the book called "Valparaiso," but in the hope that they may awaken the curiosity of some other reader, I will leave them as I found them, *i nGaeilge!*

If you are looking for a low-to-medium impact *Gaeltacht* experience that combines tension-free language learning and fascinating cultural exposure, then the Oideas Gael language and culture course in Glencolumbkille, County Donegal, is definitely for you. My wife, Shizuka, and I decided to enroll in that particular course, rather than a straight language curriculum, because of our different language levels and the multifaceted nature of the program, and it ended up being one of the most memorable trips we have ever taken.

The course is ideal both for those with no previous experience who are seeking an introduction to the land and its language and those who have studied Irish, either on their own or in a classroom situation, but who want to immerse themselves in a "live" environment where Irish is actually spoken as a native language. Shizuka rated herself "minus three" and was nervous about participating; I was completely self-taught, having learned what little I knew from books and tapes, and so my knowledge was all passive. As it turned out, neither one of us had anything to worry about, for the course was so inspiring that both of us became even more enthusiastic about pursuing our Irish studies after we got back to the States.

The school is in a remote location, not as easily accessible from Dublin or Shannon as, for example, the Connemara Gaeltacht, but that is exactly one of its drawing points. The little valley of Glencolumbkille in northwest Donegal is a picture-postcard charming locale that is the ideal spot for the Oideas Gael campus, located in the tiny village of Cashel on the Atlantic coast. The ride from Killybegs to the glen along the Slieve League peninsula is itself worth the price of the plane ticket to Ireland, with its sweeping panoramas of sea and sky, hemmed by gorgeous stretches of beaches ("strands") lying at the base of steep, dramatic cliffs.

We were greeted on our arrival by the director of the program, Liam Ó Cuinneagáin, a charismatic man of unflagging energy and exceptional organizational skills, who immediately put us at ease and drove us to our lodgings. Students can choose between sharing accommodations on the campus or staying in bed and breakfasts with local families. We wanted to be with people who spoke Irish, and so asked for a B&B, which included not only breakfast, but dinner as well.

The house where we stayed was run by a formidable presence named Máire Uí Chuinneagáin (no relation, apparently, for this name, Cunningham, is perhaps the most common name in the valley, after Ó Beirne). It was a good half-mile from the school, so we were able to take care of our exercise requirements by walking back and forth two or three times a day. Good, plain Irish fare was provided, and above all, a willingness to help us with our struggling Irish. Máire told me later, to my utter amazement, that she was not a native Irish speaker but had moved to Glencolumbkille as a teenager and had had a tough time at first with the language. You would never have known it, judging by the astounding ease and speed with which she could switch back and forth between English and Irish. Her husband Seán and their helper, a charming woman named Áine, however, were natives of the area and had spoken Irish since childhood with that northern *blas,* which takes getting used to but won me over after a short time. Our housemates were four very pleasant Irish women who lived in England, some of whom had taken the same course as many as seven times before!

Classes were held every morning and were divided into eight levels, from one (no experience with the language) to eight (near native or native ability). My teacher, Nóirín, was a young woman from Gweedore who was a native speaker of

Irish. She spoke a mile a minute and I had a great deal of difficulty understanding anything she said, but she and the rest of the class were sympathetic to my plight, and convinced me, the only *Poncán* (Yank), to remain in the class, which I at first felt was much too advanced. It was such a thrill being among Irish speakers, though, that I really didn't care what class I was in.

Emphasis was on developing our speaking skills and rein-forcing grammar. I learned a lot, but realized that all my self-study had not gotten me very far and that there is no substitute for a live classroom situation such as this. Shizuka reported that her class was relatively stress-free and that she was not, as she had feared, "the worst." It was not long before she was greeting me with *Cad é mar atá tú?* ("How are you?") and telling me to *Tóg go bog é* ("Take it easy") with the rest of them.

It is this ability of the Oideas Gael program to inspire enthusiasm in people with varying degrees of interest in the language that is one of its strongest points. We were encouraged to speak Irish as much as possible during the breaks and outside the class, although this was not always easy because of the great differences in the levels of the students, many of whom were from Ireland and had had the advantage of studying Irish in school. Many others, however, were from countries as far away as Germany and Japan, not to mention the States.

It was also somewhat of a challenge to find opportunities to use Irish in the village, despite its claim as a Gaeltacht area. The young people, especially, did not seem to feel it was "cool" to converse among themselves in Irish, and one was never sure in the shops whether our faltering efforts would be welcome or not. This is part of the neurosis that affects the language everywhere, I think, so one has to learn to live with it. The chances to speak Irish are there if you are not afraid to make a fool of yourself. (Something I have never been accused of!) This "fools rush in" attitude was responsible, I am sure, for my being selected for an interview on Raidió na Gaeltachta, the Irish-language radio station, another huge thrill.

Since our lunch was not included in the B&B arrangement, we usually ate right next door to the school at "An Chistin," an excellent eatery with a delicious menu of light fare served graciously with no waiting and, as elsewhere in Ireland, optional tipping!

In the afternoons we had our "workshops," a choice among many activities to suit every taste, from hill walking (our original choice, but when we learned it would be an hour longer than the others, and with no sign of the rain letting up, we opted for tin whistle classes!) to drama, with everything from singing (both "regular" Irish songs and in the traditional *sean-nós* style), to literature, and dancing, and others in between. This was a good way to rest from the rigors of the morning language training and to absorb some of the culture at the same time. We had loads of fun, and our tin whistle teacher, Liam Ó Néill, was also a skilled fiddler who could often be heard at the nightly "sessions" in the pubs.

As interesting and enjoyable as our days turned out to be, I feel that the entertainment provided nightly after we returned to the school from dinner was truly outstanding and in many cases unforgettable. Each night a different concert or program was presented, and each one seemed to surpass the other. It seemed unbelievable to me that people about whom I had read, whose music I had bought, or whose poetry I had read, were actually standing in front of me singing, talking, and reciting! Granted, the Gaelic arts world is a small one, but we were still mightily impressed to hear two-time *Corn Ó Riada* winner Lillis Ó Laoire singing two feet away from us at the *sean-nós* evening, and to be treated at the same time to the lovely singing of our MC, Gearóidín Bhreathnach (who also taught the *sean-nós* workshop) and performances by several of her seven children! Singer-entertainer Tadhg Mac Dhonnagáin had us all laughing and singing along with him on another evening; the famous Donegal poet Cathal Ó Searcaigh transfixed us with readings from his own works; and a group of truly talented musicians from Belfast, Ceoltóirí Rossa, had us warbling in Irish during our first Gaelic hootenanny! Another evening we went to the town auditorium, Halla Mhuire, for a performance by the local acting troupe of an Irish comedy written by Ireland's first President, Douglas Hyde, called *An Cleamhnas* (the matchmaking). Imagine the shock of recognition when the curtain went up and there in the leading role of the mother was our *bean an tí* from the B&B! She had us in stitches and afterwards, we went backstage to congratulate her, in the company of the current President of Ireland, Mary Mac Aleese, who was also spending the week with us improving her Irish.

As you can see, our days were full. If there has been little mention of the weather, it must be because we have been trying to forget how awful it was, even to the point where the locals were complaining! We did not expect the south of France, but it would have been nice to see the sun a little more often. We would like to believe that it was just bad luck for us. If you go, just think "Seattle" and you'll be fine.

No amount of rain or chilly temperatures in mid-July can diminish the charm of that little village nestled in that green, sheep-filled valley.

As the bus for Dublin pulled out early Saturday morning and stopped at the top of the hill, we turned around and gazed one more time at what we had always imagined Ireland to look like. We both let out an involuntary sigh, and vowed to go back another day.